T0311807

# Cambridge Elements ≡

Elements in the Philosophy of Ludwig Wittgenstein
edited by
David G. Stern
*University of Iowa*

# WITTGENSTEIN AND AESTHETICS

## Hanne Appelqvist
*University of Helsinki*

CAMBRIDGE
UNIVERSITY PRESS

Shaftesbury Road, Cambridge CB2 8EA, United Kingdom

One Liberty Plaza, 20th Floor, New York, NY 10006, USA

477 Williamstown Road, Port Melbourne, VIC 3207, Australia

314–321, 3rd Floor, Plot 3, Splendor Forum, Jasola District Centre,
New Delhi – 110025, India

103 Penang Road, #05–06/07, Visioncrest Commercial, Singapore 238467

Cambridge University Press is part of Cambridge University Press & Assessment,
a department of the University of Cambridge.

We share the University's mission to contribute to society through the pursuit of
education, learning and research at the highest international levels of excellence.

www.cambridge.org
Information on this title: www.cambridge.org/9781108931120

DOI: 10.1017/9781108946452

© Hanne Appelqvist 2023

This work is in copyright. It is subject to statutory exceptions and to the provisions
of relevant licensing agreements; with the exception of the Creative Commons version
the link for which is provided below, no reproduction of any part of this work may take
place without the written permission of Cambridge University Press.

An online version of this work is published at doi.org/10.1017/9781108946452
under a Creative Commons Open Access license CC-BY-NC 4.0 which permits
re-use, distribution and reproduction in any medium for non-commercial purposes
providing appropriate credit to the original work is given. You may not
distribute derivative works without permission. To view a copy of this license, visit
https://creativecommons.org/licenses/by-nc/4.0/

All versions of this work may contain content reproduced under license from third
parties. Permission to reproduce this third-party content must be obtained from these
third-parties directly.

When citing this work, please include a reference to the DOI 10.1017/9781108946452

First published 2023

*A catalogue record for this publication is available from the British Library.*

ISBN 978-1-108-93112-0 Paperback
ISSN 2632-7112 (online)
ISSN 2632-7104 (print)

Cambridge University Press & Assessment has no responsibility for the persistence
or accuracy of URLs for external or third-party internet websites referred to in this
publication and does not guarantee that any content on such websites is, or will
remain, accurate or appropriate.

# Wittgenstein and Aesthetics

Elements in the Philosophy of Ludwig Wittgenstein

DOI: 10.1017/9781108946452
First published online: January 2023

Hanne Appelqvist
*University of Helsinki*

**Author for correspondence:** Hanne Appelqvist, hanne.appelqvist@helsinki.fi

**Abstract:** This Element argues that aesthetics, broadly conceived, plays a significant role in Wittgenstein's philosophy. In doing so, it draws on the interpretative tradition that emphasizes affinities between Wittgenstein's thought and Kant's philosophy. Following the chronology of Wittgenstein's philosophical work, this Element addresses Wittgenstein's early equation between ethics and aesthetics, his middle-period discussion on the normative character of aesthetic judgments and the possibility of their justification, and his later comparison between language and music. As a whole, it traces a continuous line of thought pertaining to a non-conceptual form of encounter with reality, which is developed in close conjunction with aesthetics and contributes to Wittgenstein's understanding of language and the method of philosophy throughout his career. This Element is also available as Open Access on Cambridge Core.

**Keywords:** aesthetic judgment, ineffability, Kant, normativity, philosophical method

© Hanne Appelqvist 2023

ISBNs: 9781108931120 (PB), 9781108946452 (OC)
ISSNs: 2632-7112 (online), 2632-7104 (print)

# Contents

# 1 Introduction

Aesthetics is usually understood as the philosophical investigation of art, beauty, and taste. Standard questions within the field pertain to the essence of art, artistic and aesthetic value, aesthetic experience and judgment, and the meaning, understanding, and interpretation of artworks. Most of these themes figure in Ludwig Wittgenstein's writing, where, from 1915 onward, we find observations on aesthetic contemplation, reason-giving in aesthetics, and the nature of musical meaning and understanding. In Wittgenstein's *Nachlass*, there are also numerous remarks on composers, literary authors, poets, and, for example, the notion of a genius, testifying to his awareness of the aesthetic debates prevalent in his cultural milieu. Music in particular had a dominant role in Wittgenstein's life and thought, which is natural given his early immersion in Viennese musical life.[1]

However, in addition to its narrow disciplinary sense, the term aesthetics has a broader philosophical use. In the broad sense of the term, originating in the work of Alexander Baumgarten and underscored by Immanuel Kant's philosophical project, aesthetics refers to the investigation of the domain of sensibility in general (Baumgarten 1954, §CXVI; CPR A21/B35–36). As such, aesthetics is explicitly contrasted with the conceptual domain of logic. Sensible perception, imagination, and feeling are treated as a realm independent of and irreducible to the discursive realm of concepts, contributing to cognition on its own terms.

The two senses of "aesthetics" have natural points of overlap, because judgments about art and other objects of aesthetic appreciation are often treated as paradigm examples of judgments pertaining to sensibility. Kant too ultimately connects transcendental aesthetic as discussed in the *Critique of Pure Reason* with his account of pure judgments of taste, in spite of his initial hesitation to deem the latter worthy of transcendental investigation (CPR A21/B35fn; see Guyer and Wood 2000, xiii–xiv). Nonetheless, it is possible to address issues belonging to aesthetics in the narrow sense independently of sensibility (as in the quest for the definition of "art"), and questions pertaining to sensibility independently of philosophy of art and beauty (when investigating, e.g., the nature of visual experience).

---

[1] Wittgenstein's family was exceptionally musical and regularly hosted musical events attended by people like Johannes Brahms, Josef Joachim, Gustav Mahler, Josef Labor, and Richard Strauss. It is also indicative of the family's eminence in musical circles that when Wittgenstein's brother, the concert pianist Paul Wittgenstein, lost his right arm in the war, Maurice Ravel, Sergei Prokofiev, and Benjamin Britten composed music for the left hand specifically for him. On Wittgenstein's life and family, see Janik and Toulmin 1973; McGuinness 1988; Monk 1990; and Waugh 2008.

The ambiguity of the term contributes to the difficulty of appreciating Wittgenstein's views on aesthetics and their relevance for his philosophy. That Wittgenstein's own usage of the term oscillates between the broad and narrow senses adds to the difficulty. For example, in *Notes Dictated to G. E. Moore in Norway* in 1914, Wittgenstein alludes to Kant's distinction between transcendental aesthetic and transcendental logic. In a discussion on visual spots that may be internally related to each other either spatially or with regard to their color, he states: "We might thus give a sense to the assertion that logical laws are *forms* of thought and space and time *forms* of intuition" (NB, 118). Here, space and time as "forms of intuition" are precisely what Kant's transcendental aesthetic treats and does so independently of aesthetics narrowly conceived (CPR A 21–22/B 35–36).

The word "aesthetics" appears in Wittgenstein's notes for the first time in 1916. He writes: "Ethics must be a condition of the world, like logic. Ethics and aesthetics are one" (NB, 77). Again, the alignment of logic and the amalgamated ethics-cum-aesthetics suggests that the word is used in its broad sense. In his later philosophy, Wittgenstein connects such experiences as observing the lighting in a room, reading a sentence with a peculiar attention, and listening to music to what he calls intransitive understanding, namely, the kind a kind of understanding that cannot be discursively further explained, and even to the question of idealism and realism. These examples similarly disclose a broader understanding of the notion of aesthetics than the disciplinary sense of the term accommodates.

This is not to say that one cannot read some of Wittgenstein's remarks against the backdrop of aesthetics in the disciplinary sense. In his lectures on aesthetics in 1933 and 1938, Wittgenstein addresses the distinction between the beautiful and the agreeable, the justification of aesthetic judgments, the criteria of understanding the arts, and the cultural embeddedness of artefacts. These themes correspond to discussions prevalent in the field of aesthetics. At the same time, other topics central in mainstream aesthetics are absent from Wittgenstein's enquiry. For instance, while Wittgenstein makes observations on specific works of art, the classificatory concept of art does not inform his approach. Nor does he address the definition of the concept "art," central in mainstream aesthetics, even if the topic readily lends itself to his idea of family resemblance and has been treated by reference to it.[2] Wittgenstein's interest lies in complex and historically developing "aesthetic systems" like music and architecture, which he claims

---

[2] See Weitz 1956. For discussions on art in light of Wittgenstein's philosophy, see, for example, Wollheim 1968; Eldridge 1987; Sedivy 2016, 97–147.

should be investigated "grammatically," in a way similar to the philosophical investigation of language (LC 9:40; LA II:18).[3]

A characteristic feature of Wittgenstein's treatment of aesthetics, marking a clear contrast with mainstream analytic aesthetics, is that he does not seem to approach the topic in any systematic fashion. Notwithstanding his lectures where some aesthetic questions are discussed at more length, Wittgenstein's remarks on aesthetics and the arts typically surface in the context of other topics just to disappear from sight again. In this regard, his approach is closer to the German tradition, where the arts and especially music are allied with such core areas of philosophy as epistemology, metaphysics, and ethics. In the *Tractatus*, Wittgenstein refers to music at key moments of his explication of the picture theory of language. In *The Blue and Brown Books*, music is connected to aspect-seeing and the understanding of language. And in the *Philosophical Investigations*, music figures again as an object of comparison for the understanding of language. Some scholars have treated such interconnections as evidence of Wittgenstein's determination to bring aesthetics to bear on broader philosophical issues much in the same way as Kant did in his *Critique of the Power of Judgment*.[4] Others, by contrast, are less optimistic about relating Wittgenstein's remarks on aesthetics and the arts to his core concerns and lean toward treating them as his personal musings or cultural commentary of a nonphilosophical kind.[5]

This contribution to Elements in the Philosophy of Ludwig Wittgenstein strives to show that aesthetics plays an important role in Wittgenstein's philosophy throughout his career. In doing so, the Element draws on the interpretative tradition that emphasizes affinities between Wittgenstein and Kant.[6] I thus disagree with the traditional readings according to which Wittgenstein's

---

[3] Edited collections dedicated to Wittgenstein's aesthetics include Johannessen 1998; Allen and Turvey 2001; Gibson and Huemer 2004; Lewis 2004; Majetschak and Lütterdelfs 2007; Arbo, Le Du, and Plaud 2012; Hagberg 2017. Special issues on the theme have been published in *L'Art du Comprende* 20, 2011; *Aisthesis* 6 (1), 2013; *Ápeiron: Estudios de filosofía* 10, 2019; and *Estetika: The European Journal of Aesthetics* 57 (1), 2020.

[4] See, for example, Cavell 1969; Bell 1987; Moore 1987, 1997, 203–206; Appelqvist 2017, 2019b; Day 2017.

[5] This view is common among the representatives of the so-called traditional reading of Wittgenstein's philosophy and often reflects a strictly disciplinary understanding of aesthetics (see von Wright 1977, ixe; Hacker 1986, 101; Glock 1996, 31; Budd 2011, 775; Schroeder 2017, 612).

[6] Accounts on the strength, source, and pervasiveness of Kant's influence on Wittgenstein and the exegetical detail in which they are explicated vary across the literature. Accordingly, any given Kantian interpretation is Kantian to a greater or lesser degree. Some argue that the similarities between the two can be attributed to Schopenhauer's influence (e.g., Hacker 1986; Pears 1987; Stern 1995; Sluga 2011). Others have read Wittgenstein more directly in light of Kant's transcendental idealism. On Kant's influence on Wittgenstein's early philosophy, see Stenius 1960; Kannisto 1986; Glock 1992, 1997; Moore 1987, 2013; Appelqvist 2013, 2016. On his influence

remarks on aesthetics (and ethics) cannot be seamlessly fitted into the larger framework of his philosophy. I also contest the resolute readings that, while stressing the ethical and sometimes aesthetic import of Wittgenstein's work, reject the notion of ineffability as central for Wittgenstein's position.[7] From the Kantian viewpoint, ineffability – the principled impossibility of conceptually determining every aspect of our encounter with reality – is but a natural corollary of the essentially nonconceptual domain of aesthetics.

Reading one enigmatic philosopher with the help of another equally challenging and complex thinker has its obvious dangers. Kant's philosophy is subject to as much controversy as Wittgenstein's, and appealing to Kant always involves interpretation. Moreover, if Wittgenstein was influenced by Kant's views, as I argue, those views have been transformed and incorporated into his own project. The affinities between the two also come in degrees. Sometimes we hear but faint echoes of Kant in Wittgenstein's writing, at other times a remark by Wittgenstein reads almost as a paraphrase of Kant's text.[8] Finally, the views of both Kant and Wittgenstein have been appropriated and developed further in aesthetics and elsewhere. It is not always easy to disentangle Wittgenstein's own position from a "Wittgensteinian" position, and the same applies to Kant. I have tried to stay as close as possible to the original texts, but some of Kant's views have become so entrenched in aesthetics that it is occasionally more natural to talk more generally about Kantian views.

Wittgenstein is notoriously sparing with his references to other philosophers, including Kant. It is thus difficult to determine with certainty what the exact sources of his expressed views are. We know that Wittgenstein read *The Critique of Pure Reason* in 1918 and some of his explicit references to Kant appear already in 1914.[9] He also compares Kant favorably to Schopenhauer, and claims that Kant's method is the "right sort of approach" in philosophy (LWL, 73; Rhees 1981, 95). Such remarks would be surprising had Wittgenstein not had first-hand knowledge of Kant's philosophy. Yet, to my knowledge, there is no direct evidence of Wittgenstein reading Kant's *Critique of the Power of*

---

on Wittgenstein's later philosophy, see Cavell 1969, 1979; Williams 1981; Bell 1987; Garver 1994; Appelqvist 2017, 2018, 2019b; Ritter 2020.

[7] The resolute reading approaches the *Tractatus* as a text that employs literary techniques, thereby bringing aesthetics to bear on Wittgenstein's work. At the same time, it rejects the interpretation according to which the early Wittgenstein is committed to the idea of inexpressible logical, ethical, or aesthetic knowledge or understanding. See Diamond 1983, 1988, 2000; Kremer 2001; Conant 2002, 2005.

[8] Consider, for example, TLP 2.013 vs. CPR A24/B38; TLP 5.61 and PI §435 vs. CPR A 476/B504; PI §118–119 vs. CPR Axiii; CV, 94 [82] vs. CPR A598/B626.

[9] See McGuinness 1988, 252, 270; Monk 1990, 158. Ian Proops has argued that Wittgenstein's earliest references to Kant betray familiarity with Kant's *Prolegomena* (Proops 2004, 109; see NB, 15; TLP 6.36111).

*Judgment*, although some of Wittgenstein's ideas, such as wallpaper as an example of beauty, strike curiously close to Kant's text (see LC 9:16, 9:20; CPJ 5:229). Given the inconclusiveness of the available evidence, I am reluctant to make strong claims about the actual historical link between Kant and Wittgenstein. It is possible that some of Wittgenstein's Kantian commitments, like the distinctions between the agreeable and the beautiful, between reasons and causes, or between nature and art, have been transmitted through other thinkers. My argument is rather that, regardless of their exact mode of transmission, the affinities between Wittgenstein and Kant are too deep and pervasive to be ignored. Most importantly, I am convinced that only by reading Wittgenstein's remarks on aesthetics in light of Kant's philosophy can we understand their meaning and significance for Wittgenstein's philosophy as a whole.

The structure of this Element follows the chronological development of Wittgenstein's work, beginning from his early philosophy. The primary goal of Section 2 is to cast light on Wittgenstein's alignment of ethics and aesthetics in the context of his early philosophy. The textual evidence of the *Tractatus* is limited, but combining it with the earlier *Notebooks 1914–1916* will help to uncover central features of Wittgenstein's understanding of the perspective that aesthetics and ethics share. The section ends by relating this perspective to the overall framework of the *Tractatus*, especially to its fundamental distinction between saying and showing.

Section 3 explores Wittgenstein's most sustained discussions on aesthetics, available in the lecture notes from 1933 and 1938. Of the two sets of notes, the 1933 notes have been meticulously taken and carefully edited. The 1938 notes, while more well-known, are less reliable in this regard.[10] The key theme figuring in both sets of lectures is the nature of aesthetic judgment and the possibility of its justification. In 1933, Wittgenstein stresses the Kantian contrast between judgments of beauty and of the agreeable, arguing against the possibility of explaining aesthetics in a naturalistic fashion. In the 1938 lectures, the notion of aesthetic explanation, given by reference to reasons rather than causes, is developed further. Like Kant, whose account of beauty combines a subjective and an objective component, Wittgenstein discusses the interface between subjective reactions to aesthetic phenomena and the communally shared rules, conventions, and practices that are constitutive of those phenomena. The argumentative goal of Section 3 is to explicate how the two sides of

---

[10] See Anscombe's letter to von Wright on March 14, 1984, available at the National Library of Finland; Diamond 2005, 99.

aesthetic judgment come together in a way that anticipates Wittgenstein's mature discussion of rule-following.

Section 4 addresses Wittgenstein's comparison between language and music, a theme mentioned already in his earliest writings and becoming increasingly prominent in his later thought. The issue at stake is the constitution of meaning and the related question of understanding. We find early formulations of Wittgenstein's position in the *Brown Book* and more developed versions of the same ideas in the *Investigations*. After contextualizing Wittgenstein's remarks on musical meaning against the tradition of aesthetics, the section argues that a nonconceptual form of understanding, similar to aesthetic judgment as Wittgenstein understands it, is evoked in the *Investigations* to complement the discursive form of understanding cashed out by reference to rule-formulations.

Section 5 addresses the broader significance of aesthetics in Wittgenstein's philosophy. Starting from Wittgenstein alignment between philosophical and aesthetic investigation, it offers a preliminary analysis of the contribution of aesthetics to his conception of the method of philosophy. A central notion in this context is that of surveyable representation, which Wittgenstein develops in close proximity to aesthetics. As a whole, the interpretation defended in this Element highlights the continuities of Wittgenstein's thought from his earliest philosophical innovations to his mature understanding of language and philosophy.

## 2 Wittgenstein's Early Philosophy

### 2.1 Aesthetics and Ethics

In the *Tractatus*, ethics and aesthetics are claimed to be one (TLP 6.421). Consistent with this claim, most of Wittgenstein's early references to aesthetics appear in the context of his reflection on the purpose of life. The discussion unfolds by reference to three frameworks that, for Wittgenstein, are intimately intertwined or even identical, namely, ethics, aesthetics, and religion.[11] Indeed, it is impossible to make sense of Wittgenstein's early account of aesthetics without paying attention to what he writes about ethics and religious faith. Another caveat concerns the sources available. While Wittgenstein's 1916 notes contain a lot of material on the problem of life, the number of related remarks in the *Tractatus* is limited. It is therefore difficult to judge whether the *Tractatus*'s account of ethics and aesthetics corresponds to the one we may extrapolate from *Notebooks 1914–1916*. However, since certain key features of Wittgenstein's

---

[11] On the interconnections, see Barrett 1991; Tilghman 1991; Gmür 2000.

conception of the aesthetic judgment survive to his latest remarks, we may assume that the *Notebooks* provide a fairly reliable picture of his early approach to aesthetics.

What Wittgenstein calls the "problem of life" arises out of the tension between the contingent facts of the world and the possibility of happiness – a tension equally present in Kant's philosophical enterprise (TLP 6.521, 6.41; CPR A814/B842; CPrR 5:113; CPJ 5:176).[12] According to the *Tractatus*, the world is the totality of contingent and hence valueless facts. The picture theory of language, usually seen as the philosophical core of the *Tractatus*, leaves no other role for the subject but to picture those facts; that is, to think about how things either actually or potentially stand. The subject is a spectator of facts over which it has no control; it "does not belong to the world: rather, it is a limit of the world" (TLP 5.632; see TLP 6.373). Yet, toward the end of the book Wittgenstein suggests that, in addition to its picturing relation to the world of facts, the subject has a will (TLP 2.1, 6.423–6.43; see NB, 72–73). In contrast to valueless facts, the will is either good or bad, and this difference manifests itself in the happiness or unhappiness of the subject's world (TLP 6.423–6.43; NB, 86–87). But what does it mean for the will to be good if facts have no value? And how is it possible to reach harmony between one's will and the world, which is what happiness requires?

Wittgenstein's response to the problem is articulated by reference to a particular perspective on the world, which is distinct from the perspective of natural sciences yet available for the subject. Natural sciences operate within the domain of meaningful language, where all propositions have the general form "This is how things stand" (TLP 4.1, 4.5). Since how things stand is accidental, the facts of the world are neither good nor bad. Accordingly, the problem of life remains completely untouched even when all possible empirical questions about the world have been answered (TLP 6.52). However, there is another perspective that does not yield any thoughts or propositions. Wittgenstein calls this perspective the view *sub specie aeterni*, the "view from eternity," and suggests that the experience of value or purpose resides in that perspective (TLP 6.45).

The subject's experience of value does not correspond to thoughts or propositions in the technical sense of the *Tractatus*, because every possible thought is about empirical facts, whether possible or actual (TLP 6.42). So instead of characterizing the evaluative perspective or the experience emerging from it as a thought or a proposition, Wittgenstein speaks of *viewing* and *feeling*. He writes: "To view the world sub specie aeterni is to view it as a whole – a

---

[12] See Moore 1987; Appelqvist and Pöykkö 2020.

limited whole. Feeling the world as a limited whole – it is this that is mystical" (TLP 6.45). Rather than approaching the world as an aggregate of mutually independent and contingent facts – a complete catalogue of which is provided by the corpus of the natural sciences – the evaluative perspective takes as its object the world viewed as a limited whole (TLP 1–1.21, 4.11). As such, the world is viewed from a unique point of view that belongs to the subject as the world's limit (TLP 5.632). Accordingly, the world takes on the character of being the subject's life: the world is given to me as "*my* world," which is to say that, for the subject, the "world and life are one" (TLP 5.62–5.621). This insight falls outside the bounds of meaningful language. At the same time, it is the first step for seeing how the world of contingent facts can relate to the subject's will and to good and bad as predicates of that will (NB, 79).[13]

The perspective on the world as a unique, limited whole is equally manifest in aesthetics, ethics, and religion. While both ethics and religion, at least ordinarily understood, are directly related to the question of the value and purpose of life, the connection is not as obvious in the case of aesthetics. Yet, for Wittgenstein, aesthetics actually assumes priority over ethics and religion. This is because what he writes about the evaluative perspective echoes features that are traditionally attributed to aesthetic attitude or judgment.

Wittgenstein's identification between ethics and aesthetics emerges for the first time in 1916 as an elaboration of the claim that ethics "must be a condition of the world, like logic" (NB, 77). In the *Tractatus*, the identification is preceded by a characterization of ethics as "transcendental" (TLP 6.421).[14] From the viewpoint of Kant's philosophy, there is no essential difference between the two explications, because transcendentality just means the necessary conditions for the possibility of judging the world (CPR A56/B86). Wittgenstein's position reflects this conception: neither ethics nor logic is *about* the world of empirical facts, but condition that world. Logic conditions the world by grounding the possibility of facts including propositions. Logical form makes it possible for objects to combine together into states of affairs, and it allows thoughts and propositions to picture those states of affairs since the necessary condition for such picturing is a shared form between the picture and the pictured (TLP 2.033, 2.17). But how are we to understand the conditioning of ethics-cum-aesthetics?

---

[13] For an alternative reading of "feeling the world as a limited whole," see (Friedlander 2001, 136–144). Friedlander acknowledges the link between Kant and Wittgenstein, but overlooks the role of the notion of a world-whole in their respective accounts (cf. Stenius 1960, 223; Moore 2013, 253).

[14] In the *Notebooks*, Wittgenstein calls ethics "transcendent" (NB, 77). However, his characterization of ethics as a condition of the world implies that what he means is transcendentality rather than transcendence. This interpretation is reinforced by the mature formulation of the same point in TLP 6.421.

One way to approach the question is to start from the assumption that just as meaningful thoughts or propositions must conform to the general propositional form grounded in logic, judgments of value have a shared *form* (TLP 4.5).[15] This proposal accords with Kant's transcendental idealism: the forms of our judgments condition our judgments as well as their objects, making it possible for the two to have an internal, necessary relation (cf. TLP 2.0121; CPR A57/B81). And indeed, Wittgenstein's explanation of the oneness of ethics and aesthetics emphasizes the shared perspective from which they arise: "The work of art is the object seen *sub specie aeternitatis*; and the good life is the world seen *sub specie aeternitatis*. This is the connexion between art and ethics" (NB, 83).

At the outset, this remark might lead us to think that aesthetics refers to the "view from eternity" when directed to works of art, whereas ethics takes the world or one's life as its object. However, Wittgenstein's elaboration on the theme and his emphasis on the formal features of the perspective cast doubt on a neat separation between ethics and aesthetics even at this level of abstraction.[16]

Granted, Wittgenstein mentions the work of art as the aesthetic manifestation of the *sub specie aeterni* perspective (NB, 83; CV, 7 [5]).[17] Yet, the only concrete example of an object of aesthetic contemplation in his 1916 discussion is a mundane, everyday object:

> If I have been contemplating the stove, and then am told: but now all you know is the stove, my result does indeed seem trivial. For this represents the matter as if I had studied the stove as one among the many things in the world. But if I was contemplating the stove *it* was my world, and everything else colourless by contrast with it. (NB, 83)

The ordinariness of Wittgenstein's example serves to underscore the primacy of the perspective over its object. Instead of starting from canonical artworks as objects inspiring aesthetic contemplation, the example implies that *any* object may be seen *sub specie aeterni* and thereby acquire significance for the subject. Moreover, Wittgenstein claims the stove to *be* his world in the moment of contemplation writing that "as a thing among things, each thing is equally insignificant; as a world each one equally significant" (NB, 83). Later, in

---

[15] See Appelqvist 2013.

[16] Here, I disagree with Benjamin Tilghman, for whom Wittgenstein's claim about the oneness of ethics and aesthetics just indicates an "important similarity" (see Tilghman 1991, 45). For other readings on the oneness of ethics and aesthetics, see Barrett 1984; Collinson 1985; Wilde 2004; Janik 2007; Varga 2009.

[17] Throughout this book, I use the 1998 edition of *Culture and Value* (CV). However, references are cited from both the 1998 and 1980 bilingual editions. The reference to the 1980 edition is given in square brackets.

1930, Wittgenstein notes that viewing one's life *sub specie aeterni* is to view it as a work of art (CV, 6 [4]). It thus seems that the distinction between an object and the world is not relevant for the evaluative viewpoint, and accordingly that there is no principled difference between ethics and aesthetics.

To understand ethics as conditioning the world is to identify it with the perspective that shows the world of contingent facts as a limited whole and hence as the subject's unique life. Given that the judgments grounded in the *sub specie aeterni* perspective show anything – the totality of facts, a work of art, or a stove – as a possible "world," the distinction between ethics and aesthetics dissolves. It is the perspective itself that carries the entire weight of the judgment being a judgment of value. Given Wittgenstein's strict notion of meaningful language as the totality of pictures of possible facts, judgments of value cannot be discursively expressed. Their formal character as judgments springing from the *sub specie aeterni* perspective just shows itself. In this respect, transcendental ethics is similar to transcendental logic: both condition the world as something given to the subject, albeit in different ways.

## 2.2 The View *Sub Specie Aeterni*

A striking feature of the *sub specie aeterni* perspective is that what Wittgenstein says about it closely resembles aesthetic judgment, especially as understood in the Kantian tradition. The perspective is one of disinterested contemplation, manifest in feeling rather than thought. It does not yield knowledge about the world, yet shows its object as unique and valuable for the subject.

These very features characterize the judgment of beauty as articulated in Kant's *Critique of the Power of Judgment*. This work addresses the gulf between contingent nature and the possibility of happiness associated with morality (CPJ 5:174–176). It begins from the assumption that the world may be approached from two complementing perspectives: the discursive perspective operative in the quest for knowledge and the reflective or intuitive perspective at work in pure judgments of taste and teleological judgments. Kant's argumentative goal is to establish the legitimacy of the reflective perspective by analyzing the judgment of beauty as a merely reflective judgment where the *purposiveness* of the form of an object is felt rather than conceptually determined. Kant argues that the reflective perspective can also be adopted toward the world as a whole. In the *First Critique*, he had argued that the "world-whole" falls outside the bounds of knowledge. However, in the *Third Critique* he claims that we have the right to judge the world to be a purposive, limited whole, as long as we do not take this judgment to yield knowledge (CPR A483–484/B511–512; CPJ 5:379). And it is precisely the reflective viewpoint on the world that allows us to see the possibility of harmony between contingent nature and the will bound by the moral law.

Like Kant's judgment of beauty, Wittgenstein's example of the contemplation of the stove explicitly contrasts the *sub specie aeterni* perspective with the factual perspective that yields conceptually expressible knowledge. Since "propositions can express nothing that is higher," the perspective manifests a feature that Kant requires of pure aesthetic judgments, namely, their *nonconceptuality* (TLP 6.42; NB, 78; CPJ 5:221). It is impossible to express in language what it means for an object to be "my world," as anything I could possibly *say* about the object will be mere statements of facts (TLP 4.1; see TLP 6.42–6.421). For knowledge and indeed for meaningful thought in general, the stove is but a trivial, contingent thing. However, the *sub specie aeterni* perspective does not show the stove as a trivial thing among other things, "from the midst of them" (NB, 83). Instead, the stove is seen "from outside," not *in* space and time but "*together with* space and time" (NB, 83).

Reading the final remark alongside the 1914 reference to space and time as "forms of intuition" helps make more sense of the transcendental status Wittgenstein assigns to ethics-cum-aesthetics (NB, 118). The view from eternity transcends the spatiotemporally structured world not by turning away from the world of facts toward another transcendent realm but by changing the perspective from which those facts are seen. When the spatiotemporal order of the world is set aside and I look at something as an object of wonder rather than of empirical investigation, the potential conflict between contingent facts and my will disappears. I can see that the "facts of the world are not the end of the matter" (NB, 74). The contemplative perspective that transforms the stove into the subject's world also lies at the heart of the mystical feeling of the world as a limited whole: "Aesthetically, the miracle is that the world exists. That there is what there is" (NB, 86; TLP 6.45). For knowledge, there are no miracles, because the scientific way of looking at things is not to look at them as miracles (LE, 11). But if we wonder at the existence of the world as a whole, then the possibility of seeing that world as a miracle becomes available.

As Wittgenstein's laconic remark about the world of a happy man being different from that of an unhappy man suggests, it is something of a mystery how the switch from the perspective of thought to that of valuation is actually effected (TLP 6.43). What compels the subject to turn away from the spatiotemporal order of contingent facts and contemplate them "from outside"? Wittgenstein notes that art shows things from the right perspective (NB, 83, 86). But while it might be easier to see beauty in a poem than in a stove, art itself does not *force* any particular perspective on the viewer. It is possible to read a novel as an exercise in a foreign language or as a source of knowledge of a different culture, think about paintings as investments, or play music as an energy boost while jogging. And this just means that Wittgenstein already presupposes a specific conception of how art is to be approached, namely, by freely contemplating it.

In addition to being disconnected from conceptual thought, the *sub specie aeterni* perspective is *disinterested*. It focuses on the object without relating it to its spatiotemporal context that renders the object useful for external purposes. Accordingly, the value endowed on the object in virtue of the perspective is not relative to any specific purpose but absolute (LE, 5). While disinterestedness is, especially for Kantians, a common hallmark of the aesthetic judgment, the same is not usually taken to hold for moral judgments. Even Kant connects moral value to an interest in the realization of the highest good, which for him, can be conceptually expressed (CPJ 5:207; CPrR 5:110–113). Wittgenstein, however, extends the requirements of disinterestedness and inexpressibility to ethics. This is partly because of his conviction that facts have no value, and partly because the will is incapable of changing those facts anyway (TLP 6.373, 6.41). For Wittgenstein, the connection between the will and the facts of the world is as contingent as the facts themselves, and *absolute* value cannot be grounded in anything contingent. Hence, the only available source for the harmony required for happiness is to accept the world as it is and in this sense renounce all interest in it. For Wittgenstein, "The only life that is happy is the life that can renounce the amenities of the world. To it the amenities of the world are so many graces of fate" (NB, 81). The happy man must set aside all hope and fear, he "must have no fear. Not even in face of death" (NB, 74). Such a disinterested stance allows my will to be in harmony with the world, however it might be.

Arthur Schopenhauer, whose influence is visible in Wittgenstein's early remarks, similarly saw disinterested contemplation as the essence of the aesthetic attitude. Building on Kant's requirement that pure judgments of taste be disinterested, Schopenhauer took the aesthetic attitude to have the capacity to liberate the subject from torments caused by their insatiable will (Schopenhauer 1969, 195–200).[18] Wittgenstein's view diverges from Schopenhauer's in that he does not treat all willing as categorically bad. He sides with Kant by distinguishing between good and bad willing (see TLP 6.43; NB, 73; cf. Schopenhauer 1969, 197). Nevertheless, the liberating aspect of the aesthetic perspective is present in Wittgenstein's thought:

---

[18] On Schopenhauer's influence on the early Wittgenstein, see Hacker 1986, 81–104; Glock 1999; Jacquette 2017.

Is it the essence of the artistic way of looking at things, that it looks at the world with a happy eye?
Life is grave, art is gay.
For there is certainly something in the conception that the end of art is the beautiful.
And the beautiful *is* what makes happy. (NB, 86; italics in original)

It would be a mistake to conclude that the role of art is to produce happiness in the empirical, psychological sense of the term. For Wittgenstein, the relevant sense of happiness is an overall harmony between the subject's will and the world. Happiness is not a describable property, and insofar as it has any mark, this mark can only be a "metaphysical one, a transcendent one" (NB, 78).[19] The power of the aesthetic perspective lies in its ability to overcome the facts of the world, including one's psychological states, by abandoning the perspective that focuses on those facts *as facts*.

For Kant, the judgment of beauty serves to build a bridge between the empirical world judged by theoretical reason and the possibility of happiness arising from practical reason. According to him, "*Beauty* is the form of the *purposiveness* of an object, insofar as it is perceived in it *without representation of an end*" (CPJ 5:236). In other words, while the judgment of beauty does not allow for a conceptual specification of the purpose of the object, the *form* of the object is judged to be purposive. The object is seen *as if* a will had designed it for some purpose, which we cannot conceptually determine. The same idea of intentional causality underlies the possibility of seeing the deterministic world as a purposive world-whole. We see the world *as if* designed for man's moral vocation and hence hospitable for the pursuit of the highest good, including happiness (CPJ 5:397–400).[20]

On my reading, Kant's idea of *purposiveness* understood by reference to intentional causality marks a third point of contact between Wittgenstein's early aesthetics and Kant's position. As noted, the starting point of Wittgenstein's discussion of value is the question of the purpose of life: "What do I know about God and the purpose [*Zweck*] of life?" (NB, 72). As I read him, Wittgenstein's answer evokes the paradoxical idea of purposiveness without purpose. From the viewpoint of knowledge, life does not have any purpose. Yet, Wittgenstein praises Dostoevsky for correctly seeing that "the man is fulfilling the purpose of existence who no longer needs to have any purpose except to live" (NB, 73). This vision incorporates a sense of purposiveness without an objective purpose.

---

[19] Translation altered to match the German original: "Dies Merkmal kann kein physisches, sondern nur ein metaphysisches, ein transcendentes sein."

[20] On Kant's notion of purposiveness and intentional causality, see Guyer 1997, 48–50; Allison 2001, 120–125.

In 1930, Wittgenstein returns to the possibility of seeing one's life as purposive. He describes a conversation with Paul Engelmann, who momentarily sees his own writings as glorious and worth publishing but loses all interest in doing so when seriously considering the endeavor. According to Wittgenstein, the first experience resembles the aesthetic experience of seeing ordinary human activities on a theater stage. Watching such activities in their everyday setting makes no impression on us, but the aesthetic perspective renders them glorious and "worth contemplating, as is every life & everything whatever" (CV, 6 [4]). Referring to the *sub specie aeterni* perspective, Wittgenstein states that the "work of art compels us – as one might say – to see it in the right perspective, but without art the object is a piece of nature like any other" (CV, 7 [4]). So when Engelmann contemplates his writings from the aesthetic perspective, he is seeing his own life as "God's work of art" (CV, 6 [4]). Here, the contrast between art and nature and the possibility of seeing an object of nature *as if* designed by God are precisely what Kant's reflective perspective is ultimately supposed to ground.[21]

In short, Wittgenstein's early remarks on the *sub specie aeterni* perspective follow Kant's analysis of a judgment of beauty. Wittgenstein identifies a contemplative and disinterested perspective as the essence of all judgments of value, and suggests that this perspective bestows purpose on what, for knowledge, is contingent facts. An essential feature of the perspective is the principled impossibility of expressing in words the aspect of reality revealed by the perspective. Language can express nothing but facts, but the aesthetic perspective shows those facts not *as facts* but as an aesthetic miracle. Importantly, Wittgenstein locates the aesthetic perspective in a philosophical landscape similar to Kant's overall framework. It is offered as a way of overcoming the tension between the deterministic world of contingent facts and the possibility of happiness linked to the good exercise of the will.

The proposed reading might raise a concern typically associated with moral aestheticism: if we treat moral judgments as relevantly similar or reducible to aesthetic judgments, then we lose the binding force of ethics and fall back on radical subjectivism or relativism. In light of Wittgenstein's early philosophy, the criticism thus formulated rests on a problematic understanding of moral judgments. The strict ineffability of ethics and the contingency of facts does not leave room for judgments that would distinguish between good and bad actions in the empirical domain. For Wittgenstein, and this time in contrast with Kant, "what happens, whether it comes from a stone or from my body is neither good nor bad" (NB, 84).[22] At the same time, Wittgenstein himself treats the

---

[21]  For another reading of Wittgenstein's remark on Engelmann, see Schulte 2020.

[22]  The strict inexpressibility of ethics is a major difference between Kant and Wittgenstein and might seem to undermine the Kantianism of Wittgenstein's early ethics (see Friedlander 2001, 127–131).

amalgamated ethics-cum-aesthetics as absolutely binding, as indicated by his suggestion that ethics must carry the "coercive power of an absolute judge" (LE, 7). After equating the good will and the happy life, Wittgenstein poses the very question of the source of the binding force of ethics. But instead of providing an explanation he just implies that this is something one ought to immediately see:

> And if I *now* ask myself: But why should I live *happily*, then this of itself seems to me to be a tautological question; the happy life seems to be justified, of itself, it seems that it *is* the only right life.
> . . .
> But we could say: The happy life seems to be in some sense more *harmonious* than the unhappy. But in what sense?? (NB, 78)

I have argued that the disinterested and nonconceptual *sub specie aeterni* perspective makes the harmony between the will and the contingent world possible. In Sections 3.2 and 3.3, I will argue that such a view entails neither subjectivism nor relativism. That proposal will draw on Wittgenstein's later investigation into the grounds of attributing harmony to a musical work or performance.

## 2.3 Aesthetics and Logic

Above I claimed that aesthetics, broadly construed, is intertwined with Wittgenstein's primary philosophical concerns throughout his career. The final point I want to make about Wittgenstein's early philosophy concerns a link between his notion of logical form and the Kantian account of aesthetics. For the early Wittgenstein, logic and ethics-cum-aesthetics stand on a par by being transcendental (TLP 6.13, 6.421). I have argued this to mean that both concern a form conditioning the subject's relation to the world, whether that form is of thought or of valuation. And it is noteworthy that, just as the essentially nonconceptual aesthetic perspective, language and thought as described by the early Wittgenstein also involve an ineffable moment of *seeing*.

According to the *Tractatus*'s picture theory, meaningful propositions consist of names that stand for simple elements of reality (i.e., objects as the constituents of states of affairs). Wittgenstein calls the objects the immutable "substance of the world," which is "form and content" (TLP 2.021, 2.024–2.025).

---

In my view, Wittgenstein's position is Kantian not by following Kant's moral philosophy to its end, but rather by giving the judgment of beauty a pride of place in the attempt to reconcile the morally obligated will and the world of contingent facts – a move anticipated by Kant himself and brought to fruition by Wittgenstein's identification between ethics and aesthetics (see Moore 1987, 132–133).

The forms of objects allow them to combine with each other, thereby grounding the forms of facts and ultimately the form of the entire world. This logical form is the a priori form of any imaginable world: I could neither perceive nor imagine any fact independently of it (TLP 2.022, 5.4731). That language and reality have the same form makes the picturing of facts possible by allowing names to combine together in the way in which the elements of the pictured fact are claimed to be combined (TLP 2.151, 2.18). The referential relations between names and objects, in turn, enable the proposition to "touch reality" and express its empirical content unambiguously (TLP 2.1514–2.1515, 3.25).

One of Wittgenstein's key claims is that the form shared by language and reality cannot be expressed in language. According to him:

> Propositions cannot represent logical form: it is mirrored in them.
> What finds its reflection in language, language cannot represent.
> What expresses *itself* in language, *we* cannot express by means of language.
> Propositions *show* the logical form of reality.
> They display it. (TLP 4.121)

While conditioning facts, logical form itself is not a fact. Accordingly, it cannot be expressed but rather "expresses *itself*" in structured facts, whether linguistic or nonlinguistic (TLP 4.121; see TLP 2.033, 3.14). And this just means that the subject's relation to the formal (internal) properties of facts, springing from logical form, is not mediated by concepts. Instead, those properties are *directly seen* in the facts. Wittgenstein suggests that we could call internal properties *features* of facts "in the sense in which we speak of facial features" (TLP 4.1221). As will become clear once we turn to Wittgenstein's work in the 1930s, these characterizations of the formal aspect of reality imply a connection to aesthetics broadly conceived. In his later work, a similar claim about a phenomenon resisting discursive explanation and "expressing itself" appears repeatedly in connection with aesthetic phenomena such as music. Moreover, one of Wittgenstein's main objects of comparison for the formal features of aesthetic, sensible phenomena is that of facial features (see, e.g., BBB 158–185; PI §§526–539).

In the *Tractatus*, Wittgenstein illustrates internal properties by the example he had raised already in 1914 in relation to "forms of intuition," namely, the internal relation between two shades of a color (NB, 118). According to him, "it is unthinkable" that two shades of the color blue would not stand in the "internal relation of lighter to darker" (TLP 4.123). That some judgments about colors would have an a priori status similar to the status of logical propositions, though consistent with his claim about space, time, and color as "forms of objects," is striking (TLP 2.0251, 3.02, 5.4731). So is the implication that the subject's relation to the internal relation between two shades of color is one of *direct seeing*. We find a similar idea in Kant's transcendental aesthetic, specifically in his treatment of pure intuition of geometrical truths. For Kant, the three-dimensionality of space cannot be demonstrated from concepts, nor does it depend on the empirical content of our representations. Rather, we judge with apodictical certainty that space is three-dimensional, based on the pure intuition that only three lines can intersect at right angles in one point. The three-dimensionality of space is thus something we see or "intuit" directly, without the mediation of concepts. Put in terms of a distinction Kant evokes in *Prolegomena* and later applies in the *Third Critique*, geometrical judgments are *intuitive*. The operative contrast is *discursive*, which refers to empirical judgments that rely on concepts that determine intuitions under their scope (P 4:281–286; CPJ 5:406).

In the Tractarian view, meaningful propositions display logical form, but they also have empirical content, which calls for a comparison between what the proposition *says* and how things actually stand (TLP 3.13, 4.024, 4.5). Accordingly, when dealing with ordinary propositions, our attention is directed to the content rather than the form of the proposition. But there are also propositions that *show* logical form independent of any empirical content. Tautologies do not *say* anything about empirical reality, yet they show their own form and thereby the formal properties of the world (TLP 6.1–6.12, 6.124). Moreover, to recognize a tautology as a tautology, Wittgenstein claims, we can use an "intuitive method," which consists of a pictorial presentation of the truth-combinations of the propositions' truth-arguments (TLP 6.1203). Wittgenstein's main example of tautologies is propositions of logic, but his treatment of mathematical propositions follows along the same lines. Mathematical equations are "pseudo-propositions" rather than propositions proper, as they neither represent states of affairs nor express thoughts (TLP 6.2–6.22). Again, the point reflects the *Tractatus*'s core idea that the form of the world must be directly seen and cannot be discursively explained in a metalanguage as Russell – to Wittgenstein's annoyance – optimistically suggested as a solution to the ineffability of logical form (see TLP, xxii; TLP 2.18).

While it is difficult to know what exactly Wittgenstein has in mind by calling his method intuitive, it is noteworthy that in the 1933 lectures he brings up the distinction between intuitive and discursive perspectives and explains it in a manner consistent with Kant's usage of the terms. Discussing his novel notion of a grammatical system, developed to overcome problems to which the *Tractatus*'s atomistic conception of elementary sentences led, he notes that meaning can be approached in two different ways. The first is an intuitive approach that takes "something in as a whole at a glance"; the second is the discursive way of looking at meaning as use in a calculus that can be taught to another (LC 8:59). He also notes that the grammatical investigation of the word "not" is not like the investigation of the physical world but more like the investigation of the geometry of a visual field (LC 5:75). These remarks indicate that not just objects of aesthetic contemplation and geometry but also a grammatical system can be viewed from a nondiscursive perspective that focuses on the formal features of the system. The seeds of this idea, I want to claim, are already in the *Tractatus*, where the form of a tautology and the internal relation between two colors can be seen but not said.

The link between logic and aesthetics is visible throughout the *Tractatus* also in a concrete way, because Wittgenstein evokes music at key moments of explaining his notion of logical form. Logical form is first introduced in relation to objects that are form and content (TLP 2.023, 2.025). While refusing to give concrete examples of the objects, Wittgenstein illustrates their formal essence by reference to notes. Like objects whose forms make it possible for them to combine in states of affairs, notes "must have some pitch" that allows them to come together as musical themes (TLP 2.0131). The second instance of Wittgenstein's appeal to music arises in relation to the articulate character of a proposition. Logical form grounds the possibility of structure, which is the hallmark of both nonlinguistic and linguistic facts (TLP 2.033, 2.141). Wittgenstein's explanation of this idea goes as follows: "A proposition is not a blend of words. – (Just as a theme in music is not a blend of notes.) A proposition is articulate" (TLP 3.141).[23] Just as the internal relations between the notes of a scale make the overall structure (shape or pattern) of the theme possible, the structure of the proposition rests on logical form. Finally, in explaining the isomorphism between language and reality, Wittgenstein's example is once again from the realm of music:

> A gramophone record, the musical idea, the musical notation, and the sound-waves, all stand to one another in the same internal depicting relation that holds between language and the world.
> They all share their logical construction. (TLP 4.014)[24]

On my reading, these references to music are directly related to Wittgenstein's contrast between *saying* something about the world and the form, required for the possibility of saying, just *showing* itself.

The purest example of logical form showing itself is a tautology, because it does not have any empirical content. The same is true of music. Notes do not

---

[23] Wittgenstein uses the terms "tune" (in English), "Melodie," and "musikalische Thema" interchangeably. See, for example, NB 40; NB 41 vs. TLP 3.141; BBB 166, 167; CV 54 [47]; Wittgenstein 2022, 188–197.

[24] Here I use the new translation by David Stern, Joachim Schulte, and Katia Saporiti, forthcoming from Cambridge University Press. I diverge from their translation by rendering "Notenschrift" as "musical notation" instead of "the written music."

refer to any objects, and musical themes do not picture states of affairs. In 1915, Wittgenstein expresses the point explicitly. According to him, "musical themes are in a certain sense propositions" (NB, 40). However, instead of being like ordinary propositions that say something about the empirical world, "a tune is a kind of tautology, it is complete in itself; it satisfies itself" (NB, 40). Like propositions of logic that only reveal the form necessary for the possibility of thought and reality, the tune shows its form. In this way, then, Wittgenstein's early references to music make the key idea of the *Tractatus*, namely, the idea of *seeing* logical form independently of empirical content intuitively available.[25]

## 3 The Middle Period

### 3.1 The Transition

It is an often repeated claim that one's philosophical conception of the nature of aesthetic judgment reflects one's personal aesthetic preferences. The Kantian account in particular is seen as motivated by fondness for formalistically oriented art over representational and emotive artistic expression. While merely suggestive from the philosophical point of view, such a correlation is detectable in Wittgenstein's case. He expresses reservations about the value of Mendelssohn's and Mahler's music, praises the skill and sobriety of the musical thinking of Brahms, and tries his hand at modernist architecture.[26] The aesthetic ideal of a "certain coolness" reflected in these examples finds an equally poignant manifestation in the *Tractatus* (CV, 4 [2]). A work aimed at "crystal-line purity," with every remark polished to aesthetic perfection even at the expense of intelligibility, the *Tractatus* is a formally unified whole that "satisfies itself" (PI §107; NB, 40). It is thus not surprising that the *Tractatus* has been compared to both music and architecture.[27] After completing the book, Wittgenstein gives up philosophy for a decade.

After returning to Cambridge in 1929, Wittgenstein begins lecturing under the title "Philosophy." G. E. Moore's lecture notes from 1930 to 1933 give us a vivid picture of Wittgenstein's philosophical thought in action during this

---

[25] See Gmür 2000, 151–158. The interpretation I am proposing is directly opposed to that of Janik and Toulmin, who claim that "Only art can express moral truth, and only the artist can teach the things that matter the most in life.... To be concerned merely with form, like the aesthetes of the 1890s, is to pervert art. So in its own way, the *Tractatus* is every bit as much a condemnation of *l'art pour l'art* as Tolstoy's *What is Art?*" (Janik and Toulmin 1973, 197; for Wittgenstein's own assessment of Tolstoy's theory, see CV 67 [58–59]). On my reading, art does not express any *truths*, and what it shows is precisely concerned with form.

[26] For characteristic expressions of Wittgenstein's aesthetic preferences, see, for example, CV, 4, 18, 27, 29, 40, 43, 76–77 [2, 21, 23, 25, 35, 37–38, 67].

[27] See Stenius 1960, 5; Hyman 2001, 146–151.

so-called middle period of his philosophy. The problems covered in the lectures correspond to those he thought he had solved in the *Tractatus*, including linguistic meaning, relation between thought and reality, and the nature of philosophy. Now the questions are treated by reference to the notions of grammar, games, and conventional uses of language, familiar from Wittgenstein's mature philosophy.

A central notion of Wittgenstein's middle period, marking an important difference with the *Tractatus*'s atomistic picture theory of meaning, is that of grammatical system. A word, he now claims, has meaning only in a system constituted by grammatical rules. While the idea may not seem different from his early account, according to which names have meaning only in the context of propositions, Wittgenstein's extension of the context principle to proposi- tions changes the picture (TLP 3.3). In the *Tractatus*, Wittgenstein had claimed that elementary propositions are independent of one another, but now he argues that propositions too can only be understood in the context of a grammatical system (TLP 2.061, 4.21–4.211, 6.3751; LC 5:35). Another, related Tractarian assumption Wittgenstein abandons is that of immutable objects as the world's substance. The mistake in his early requirement of a unique analysis of every proposition, intended to reveal referential connections between names and simple objects, was to confuse logical with a chemical analysis – a confusion that actually violated the *Tractatus*'s own dictum that the method of philosophy is qualitatively different from that of the natural sciences (TLP 3.25, 4.111; LC 5:96, 6:17).

A third point of divergence from his early account pertains to Wittgenstein's conception of the subject. The subject of the *Tractatus* is a solitary, even solipsistic self, placed in the world as the eye in its visual field (TLP 5.62– 5.633). The willing subject is an equally solitary observer of the world, even if the perspective of observation differs from that of propositional thought. By adopting the "artistic way of looking at things … it looks at the world with a happy eye" (NB, 86). In the 1930s, the idea of a unique point of view to which the world is given disappears along with the related notion of a universally valid form of any imaginable world (TLP 2.022). Gradually, the "I" of the *Tractatus* gets replaced by a "we," and the logical form given in the forms of objects gets replaced by grammatical rules that have no other foundation except use (LC 4:30–33).

In spite of these differences, some aspects of Wittgenstein's early position remain intact. He still adheres to his early view that the natural sciences and philosophy are qualitatively different kinds of enterprises (LC 5:1; see TLP 4.111). He still endorses the contrast between expressed contingencies and logical/grammatical necessities grounding the possibility of expression:

"Language always expresses one fact as opposed to another: never expresses what could not be otherwise – never, therefore, what is essential to the world" (LC 5:28; see TLP 2.0121). And he still connects logic/grammar to the ineffable "boundary of language" where "we can't ask anything further" (LC 5:28; see TLP 5.61). In consonance with his early view that logical form cannot be conceptually articulated, Wittgenstein takes grammar to lie beyond the requirement of discursive justification. We cannot justify grammatical rules by giving reasons, because every meaningful utterance already presupposes grammar (LC 5:54, 5:63, 5:88, 7:2; see TLP 5.473). In this respect, the autonomous status of grammar resembles that of the *Tractatus*'s logical form.

Each of these points, outlined in the context of his developing account of language, bears on Wittgenstein's treatment of aesthetics. The lectures of May term 1933 address aesthetics, ethics, and religion, thus bringing the 1930–3 set of lectures to a conclusion in the same landscape that is considered on the final pages of the *Tractatus*. However, in contrast with his early remarks whose focal point was the problem of life, Wittgenstein now directs his attention to aesthetic judgments and their justification, mentioning religion and ethics only in passing. In their stead, the formal aspect of language that lends itself to immediate seeing without the mediation of concepts becomes more prominent. Even so, it is still possible to see a connection between Wittgenstein's treatment of aesthetics and the "willing subject," albeit that now the connection is cashed out by reference to reason-giving that distinguishes intentional terminology and hence rational agency from the causal mechanism of natural laws.

## 3.2 The Beautiful and the Agreeable

Wittgenstein's first set of lectures on aesthetics opens with a reminder of his new approach to meaning: "I stress the point of view which says: to know meaning is to know use" (LC 8:59). The meaning of a word is neither an object nor a feeling that the use of the word produces in us. And, while determined by grammar, the meaning of a word is not reducible to a list of grammatical rules either. This latter conception only arises due to our tendency to think of meaning as an entity to which we can point. Wittgenstein mentions "God" and "soul" as expressions easily misunderstood because of this very tendency. Rather than treating such words as referential or statements like "The Lord is my shepherd" as expressing facts (entailing that I am a sheep, say), we should investigate them grammatically. This means that we should look at the actual uses of words and sentences in the contexts to which they belong (LC 8:77). The contextual use of religious expressions reveals that they are not empirical, let alone scientific. While expressed in terms of Wittgenstein's new approach to language, the overall point is not far off from his early treatment of religious expressions. After all, in the *Tractatus*, Wittgenstein deemed religious notions to lie outside the scope of empirical language and in his Lecture on Ethics claimed them to be allegorical expressions of experiences of absolute value (LE, 9).

Wittgenstein extends the rejection of the referential understanding of word meaning to "good," dismissing the idea of the good as a property (LC 9:2). However, he quickly reverts to themes that are more readily understood as belonging to aesthetics. He states: "Practically everything I say of 'beautiful' applies in a slightly different way to 'good,'" thereby offering a new version of his early alignment between ethics and aesthetics (LC 9:18; see LE, 4; LA I:1). The bond between the two is now explained by reference to the grammar of the words "good" and "beautiful." According to Wittgenstein, the different ways in which the words are used need not have anything in common any more than the more familiar example of "game," because the "way in which you use 'good' in particular case is <u>partly</u> defined by the topic you're talking of" (LC 9:3). Similarly, it is a mistake to think of the word "beautiful" as referring to a single property or a set of properties that all things called beautiful have in common (LC 9:13; see LA 1:1). The role of the philosopher, then, is not to look for essentialist definitions for these concepts, but simply describe the uses of these words (LC 9:17, 9:19; see LA I:8, I:13). The contextual use of the words, seen against the background of an entire culture, is what bestows them with meaning (LC 9:2; LA I:26; PI §66; Z §164).

We might reasonably expect Wittgenstein's new descriptive approach to deliver empirical case studies of the diverse situations in which people talk about the arts and other objects of aesthetic appreciation.[28] However, as the discussion of what he claims to be standard aesthetic conversations progresses, it becomes clear that Wittgenstein's approach is not exactly neutral when considered against the tradition of aesthetics. It is not only that he unequivocally rejects the project of determining the essence of beauty, irrefutably central in the discipline of aesthetics. He also dismisses historically influential expression and arousal theories of art, which locate the content of artworks in the emotive mental states of the artists or the audience, respectively. Most importantly, he discards in the strongest possible terms the naturalistic approach to aesthetics that seeks to explain aesthetic judgments or properties by reference to psychology or evolution – a position discussed in Cambridge in the 1930s and still very influential in mainstream aesthetics (see LC, 348 fn43). According to Wittgenstein, "In Aesthetic investigations the one thing we're not interested

---

[28] If this were the case, aesthetic issues would indeed "belong to art criticism, rather than philosophy," as suggested by Severin Schroeder (Schroeder 2017, 612).

in is causal connections; whereas the one thing we are interested in <u>Psychology</u> is causal connections" (LC 9:22–23).

Besides, Wittgenstein's positive contribution to aesthetics still has a clear Kantian ring. First, the very starting point of Wittgenstein's lectures on aesthetics echoes Kant's analysis of beauty. Kant too begins his analysis by denying that beauty is a conceptually determinable property of objects. Although the way in which we speak of the beautiful looks as if we attributed a property of beauty to certain objects and thus made judgments *about* those objects, this appearance is deceptive. Since the judgment of beauty does not involve concepts – required for judgments about empirical reality – it cannot objectively determine any empirical properties. The judgment of beauty is instead grounded in the subject's feeling of pleasure or displeasure in the contemplation of the form of the object. This is what Kant means by calling the judgment of beauty "aesthetic," contrasting it with "cognitive" judgments that have conceptually determined empirical content (CPJ 5:203, 5:211).

Second, given his rejection of the realist understanding of beauty as a property shared by a specific class of objects such as artworks, it is natural to read Wittgenstein as addressing a particular class of judgments. This interpretation is corroborated by Wittgenstein's explicit use of the notion of aesthetic judgment in 1935 and 1938 (LA I:15; BBB, 178). Moreover, while music especially, and to some extent literature, poetry, and architecture figure in his remarks, Wittgenstein's approach to potential candidates for aesthetic appreciation continues to be markedly inclusive: "everything whatever" may be judged aesthetically, as he noted already in 1930 (CV, 6 [4]). His examples include not just artworks and fields of art but also phenomena such as the choosing of wallpaper, tailoring, and arrangement of flowers in a flower bed (LC 9:14, 9:16, 9:20; BBB, 178; LA I:13).

Third, like Kant and in contrast to empiricist aesthetics, Wittgenstein argues that aesthetic judgments are not mere sentiments or feelings of approbation. He repeatedly ridicules psychological explanations of aesthetic judgments and claims that endorsing naturalism would mean nothing short of the end of aesthetics (LC 9:27). In 1933, Wittgenstein makes the point by reference to the characteristically Kantian distinction between judgments of the beautiful and of the agreeable, declaring that "'Beautiful' ≠ 'agreeable'" (LC 9:26). This contrast originates in the *Third Critique*, which begins by distinguishing pure judgments of taste from empirically conditioned judgments of the agreeableness of tastes, smells, and isolated colors. For Kant, both judgment types are "aesthetic" in the sense of pertaining to sensibility, but only pure judgments of taste carry a legitimate claim to necessity. We do not expect others to agree with our judgments of the agreeableness of wine or coffee, because such likings reflect our subjective idiosyncrasies. Hence, while beauty and the agreeable alike give rise to pleasure, the modal status of the judgments is different. The agreeable has an *actual* relation to pleasure, whereas the judgment of the beautiful claims that relation to be *necessary* (CPJ 5:236).[29]

Wittgenstein's usage of the term agreeable [*angenehm*] corresponds to its Kantian sense of being an empirically conditioned response of liking and hence "*merely* subjective" (BBB, 48; see CPJ 5:206). Also, his examples of the agreeable, such as the smell of a flower, the taste of coffee or roast beef, and isolated colors, match those employed by Kant (LC 9:13–26; LA II:1–3; CPJ 5:212). For Kant, such features belong to the material side of the object and elicit empirically conditioned responses in us. By contrast, the universally valid judgment of beauty concerns features that manifest a priori forms of intuition, such as the design of a painting or the formal structure of a musical composition (CPJ 5:223–226).

Fourth, like Kant, Wittgenstein juxtaposes the agreeable with the formal features of objects of aesthetic appreciation. He states:

> So to say *King Lear* is "agreeable" is like saying a chair has a smell. *King Lear* is a <u>very</u> complex experience, & this is about the least important thing you could say about it.
>
> But now you might say: Surely people who have said that the beautiful is the agreeable, can't have been such absolute asses as to overlook this? There must be <u>some</u> truth in it.
>
> Suppose one talks of a beautiful color. To say this has 100 meanings, & which way we use it depends on what we're talking about. If I say of a flower "Isn't this a marvellous colour?" I mean something quite different from if I shew a painted pattern, where it may mean "is good for a wall-paper." (LC 9:16)

This passage confirms Kant's analysis of the difference between the agreeable and the beautiful. While smells and isolated colors may be pleasing, only form opens up the possibility of free contemplation. Wittgenstein's choice for an example of the latter, namely, a pattern suitable for wallpaper, is all the more striking given that Kant is famous for using the very same example and has been ridiculed for doing so (CPJ 5:229; see LC 9:20). But if the objective is to illustrate how form can be seen as purposive without any purpose, then it is hard to find a better example. Absolute music, discussed extensively by Wittgenstein and mentioned by Kant as an example of free beauty, is a similarly germane

---

[29] Interestingly, both Henry Allison and Paul Guyer interpret Kant's argument as an appeal to linguistic usage, thus foreshadowing Wittgenstein's later approach: unlike expressions of the agreeable, the *language* of beauty is inherently normative (Guyer 1997, 119–123; Allison 2001, 103–104).

example of formal purposiveness that does not succumb to conceptual explanations (CPJ 5:229).[30]

In general, Wittgenstein's remarks on art draw attention to the shapes, patterns, rhythms, and tempo of music and poetry (LC 9:16; LA I:12, II:9).[31] Juxtaposing the smell of a flower with the color patterns of a flower arrangement, he argues that only the latter allows for a more elaborate aesthetic discussion. Although both may cause a "pleasant sensation," only in the latter case do "you enjoy a shape, in the sense in which the shape enters into the enjoyment" (LC 9:13–14; see BBB, 178; LA II:3). In this regard, the aesthetic judgment of the flower arrangement behaves like the expression of fear. We may experientially corroborate that the cause of my fear is overtiredness, but it is not the overtiredness that I fear. The intentional object of my fear, to which I refer as my reason for fear, is something entirely different, like a thunderstorm or a virus. Just as the intentional object of fear is partly constitutive of my fear, the shape of the flower arrangement is constitutive of the judgment of its beauty.

It is important to notice that the sharp contrast between the beautiful and the agreeable does not tally with empiricist aesthetics. For the empiricists, aesthetic judgments are instinctive and natural, if cultivable, responses to objects of aesthetic appreciation. So although the judgments of the Humean good critic are meant to rely on practice and an unprejudiced mind, empiricists have no resources to draw a principled difference between culinary judgments, on the one hand, and beauty, on the other. For them, both eventually rely on our natural capacity of taste. By contrast, Kantians deny that the validity of judgments of beauty could rest on an empirical regularity in our responses. They also deny that experts have the final say in matters of aesthetic value. Unlike empirical judgments, where communal agreement or the testimonies of epistemic peers may suffice for warranting a belief, the judgment of beauty is autonomous. It is free in the negative sense of being independent of external, empirical causes, but also in the positive sense of relying on the subjects' aesthetic self-determination and ability to judge for themselves (CPJ 5:281–284). I cannot make a judgment of beauty by imitating others, for I have to rely on my *own* subjectively felt pleasure or displeasure in judging the object (CPJ 5:212–213, 287).

Yet, while grounded in my subjective response to something particular, Kant argues that the judgment of beauty has universal validity. For insofar as my

---

[30] Neither Kant nor Wittgenstein uses the term "absolute music" (i.e., music without text or program). However, Kant's text clearly indicates that he refers to music without extramusical subject matter. Wittgenstein, in turn, expresses reservations about the possibility of smoothly uniting the text with the musical form and focuses on the formal features of music (see RPP1 §545; Wittgenstein 2022, 90).

[31] The centrality of formal features of art for Wittgenstein has been discussed in, for example, Schroeder 2001; Schulte 2004; Appelqvist 2019a.

judgment is based on the disinterested contemplation of the form of the object, I have eliminated all material and *merely* subjective grounds of the judgment. Kant stresses that when making a judgment of beauty, I am not *predicting* that others will agree. The claim that others, too, will feel pleasure in the contemplation of the form is rather a normative *demand* (CPJ 5:212–213). These Kantian assumptions, I argue, motivate Wittgenstein's remarks on aesthetics since the 1930s and are relevant for his later account of language and philosophy.

Harold Ursell, a mathematician who attended Wittgenstein's lectures, apparently suggested that since the only method of deciding whether something is beautiful is by experiencing the object, the issue must have something to do with psychology. Wittgenstein is quick to reject the proposal. According to him, the situation in aesthetics is "more like solving a mathematics problem" (LC 9:29). Granted, we may collect statistical data of people's preferences and produce an empirical account thereof, perhaps similar to the account Wittgenstein himself pursued with his empirical experiments on the effects of rhythm in music in 1912–13.[32] But even at their best, such experiments only yield statistical generalizations of causal connections between sets of notes and subjective feelings. At worst, the results are idiosyncratic associations, like "it makes me feel like a butterfly with a pin through me" or "it reminds me of my grandmother" (LC 9:40). In both cases, the connection between music and its effect remains external, not relevantly related to music. In conformity with his early view that appeals to the Kantian insight of beauty's formal purposiveness without a conceptually determinable purpose, Wittgenstein rejects all external explanations of aesthetic value. He notes: "Suppose you find a bass too heavy – that it moves too much; you aren't saying: If it moves less, it will be more agreeable to me. That is [sic] should be quieter is an end in itself, not a means to [an] end" (LC 9:20).

As indicated by his alignment between aesthetics and mathematics, Wittgenstein underscores the normativity of aesthetics. He states:

> The question of Aesthetics is not: Do you like it? But, if you do, why do you?
> Is "This bass moves too much" a psychological statement? Is it about human beings?
> If we ever we come to: I like this; I don't, there is an end of Aesthetics; & then comes psychology. (LC 9:27)

Rather than making a statement of actual fact, my aesthetic judgment of the bass line makes a normative claim about how the base line *should* be constructed.

---

[32] On Wittgenstein's empirical experiments with rhythm, see Guter 2020.

In addition to warranting the question "Why?" and hence a demand of justification, it also demands agreement from others: "When I say 'This bass moves too much' I don't mean merely 'It gives me such & such an impression,' because if I did I should have to be content with the answer 'It doesn't give me that impression'" (LC 9:28). In aesthetics, Wittgenstein argues, we are not content with such an answer. In the culinary domain, we accept differences of taste without thinking more about them. But if you fail to recognize the aesthetically troubling feature in the bass line, there is more at stake. I take my judgment to carry a force different from a mere personal preference and feel the pressure to justify my judgment. This is to say, fifth, that Wittgenstein's reasons for emphasizing the difference between the beautiful and the agreeable align with Kant's argument that there are judgments about the sensible domain that make a legitimate claim to necessity and hence, with right, demand consent from others.

So even though aesthetic judgments involve personal experiences, they cannot be explained by means of psychology. According to Wittgenstein, "If this were all, Aesthetics would be a matter of taste" (LC 9:26). In this context, a "matter of taste" signifies merely subjective feelings of liking and disliking with no compelling force to make others consider them worth adopting. In the *Blue Book*, Wittgenstein uses the expression in this very sense. Noting that knowledge based on personal experiences seems to lack reliability and solidity, he points out that we are inclined to treat it as "subjective" in a derogatory sense, "as when we say that an opinion is *merely* subjective, a matter of taste" (BBB, 48). However, he argues, the conclusion that personal experience cannot have any authority rests on a misleading analogy arising from our language, similar to the case of thinking that the floor on which we stand is not solid because it consists of electrons. Contrary to the received view of Wittgenstein's later thought, personal experiences need not be *merely* subjective. This is, of course, the very point of Kant's distinction between the agreeable and the beautiful. While both are grounded in personal experiences, the former are merely subjective, whereas the latter are universally valid in spite of their subjective ground in virtue of being grounded in disinterested contemplation of form.

Despite the fact that the notion of the beautiful fades into the background in Wittgenstein's later remarks on aesthetics, he never abandons his critical stance on the reduction of the aesthetic to agreeableness. As late as in 1947, he writes:

> The "necessity" with which the second thought succeeds the first. (Overture to Figaro.) Nothing could be more idiotic than to say it is "*agreeable*" to hear one after the other. – But the paradigm according to which all this is *right* is certainly obscure. "It is the natural development." You gesture with your hand, would like to say: "of course!" (CV, 65 [57]; translation altered)

As implied by Wittgenstein's verdict on the idiocy of the appeal to the agreeable, merely subjective feelings of pleasure fail to account for the normativity of aesthetic judgment marked by the terms "necessity" and "right." At the same time, we are at a loss about the paradigm or norm that would ground the normativity involved. The aesthetic judgment suggests that there must be a standard of judgment, but when trying to pin that standard down, we hit a wall (BBB, 166; see LC 9:33; LA III:5).[33] So if we are neither talking about our merely subjective feelings of liking nor have an objectively established paradigm of aesthetic correctness at hand, then how can we account for the normativity of aesthetics? – A question not unlike the question of why I should live happily (NB, 78).

## 3.3 Aesthetic Normativity

Even granting that aesthetic judgments' reliance on personal experience does not threaten their validity, provided they are properly formed, we may still wonder how such judgments relate to problem-solving in mathematics. What could possibly be the relevant similarity between mathematical and aesthetic investigation?[34] Here, Wittgenstein's notion of a grammatical system becomes especially relevant. A grammatical system consists of rules that govern the uses of words and sentences (LC 6:8). It is an ordered whole that one grasps in understanding the roles that the different parts of the system have within it (LC 5:33). The notion of a system is equally central in Wittgenstein's understanding of aesthetics. Referring to his own empirical experiments with rhythm, he declares them "useless" precisely because they failed to yield what he was looking for, namely, "utterances inside an aesthetic system" (LC 9:40). For just as words and sentences become meaningful only within the grammatical system to which they belong, aesthetic problems and solutions thereof emerge only within an aesthetic system. This is because there are grammatical and hence normative relations within such a system, similar to the relations that hold between questions and answers, judgments and their justifications, and fear or hope, say, and their intentional objects. Grammatical relations are necessary in that they could not fail to obtain: a question is in part constituted by the range of possible answers, a judgment by the reasons one can evoke to support it, and so on.

The alignment between grammatical and aesthetic systems is particularly salient in Wittgenstein's treatment of his favorite aesthetic example, music. Like numbers that do not refer to any mathematical objects, musical notes and chords

---

[33] On Kant's quest for such a standard for judgment in general, see Floyd 1998.

[34] On Wittgenstein's conception of mathematical investigation, see Floyd 2000 and Säätelä 2011.

do not stand in a referential relation to nonmusical objects. Nor do cadences, melodies, or musical works represent facts or events. Rather, they become meaningful in virtue of having a rule-governed use in the musical system to which they belong (see BBB, 1–5). In accordance with the inherent normativity of a grammatical system, Wittgenstein claims that a book of harmony does not contain any references to psychology, but makes normative statements such as "you mustn't make this transition" (LC 9:15). And the aesthetic judgments we make about music employ words such as "correct," "right," "wrong," and even "necessary," thus marking the normative force attached to these judgments (LC 9:19, 9: 39; see LA I:8, I:17). So the pressing question is, what counts as the criterion of correctness to which musicians in Wittgenstein's opinion refer? What kinds of reasons can one evoke to justify such claims as "This bass moves too much" or that "This note is absolutely necessary"? (see LC 9:28, 9:39).

Thinking of our ordinary understanding of mathematical problem-solving, a ready answer to the question of justification in aesthetics would appeal to the rules constitutive of the relevant aesthetic system. In music, such rules include the rules of harmony and counterpoint, mentioned repeatedly by Wittgenstein. Hence, we might say, for example, that not closing a cadence on the tonic chord is a mistake or that using notes that belong to the scale in which the melody is written is according to the rules, thus appealing to the conventional uses of musical elements in the context of Western tonal music. However, a closer look at Wittgenstein's notion of grammar in general, and of aesthetic judgment in particular, shows that the situation is not as straightforward. In fact, it may be less straightforward in mathematics as well, as Wittgenstein's discussion of the student learning a mathematical series suggests (PI §§143–155). While it is undeniable that Wittgenstein gives pride of place for rules in the quest for a justification of an aesthetic judgment, the rule-formulations of harmony textbooks do not resolve the issue exhaustively. The reasons for this arise from Wittgenstein's conception of the rules themselves, but also from the contribution of the subject to the judgment. The latter, I will argue, is indispensable for understanding the nature of aesthetic judgments.

Already in 1933, Wittgenstein notes that the rules of language can be changed and abandoned along the way, albeit that "if we change them, we can't use them in this way" (LC 5:88; see LC 9:1). The rules need not be explicitly formulated to serve the function of constituting meaning. Nor do we have to explicitly think of the rules governing the use of words to use them successfully (LC 8:41–42). Most importantly, every chain of justifications by reference to rule-formulations ultimately comes to an end, as Wittgenstein repeatedly reminds us, calling that end of discursive justifications a "great event" (LC 5:28). These points apply to and are even more visible in aesthetics. I will follow Wittgenstein's lead in using music as my primary example of aesthetic normativity, but his remarks on poetry and architecture are consistent with the emerging picture (see, e.g., LC 9:23, 9:45–46; LA I:12, 17).

The first thing to note is that, like rules of grammar in general, the rules of a musical system are not laws of nature but develop and change in musical practices as a result of human activity. Mentioning examples from different periods of the Western tradition from modal to romantic music, Wittgenstein acknowledges the potential difficulty of understanding music from a different culture or period. Given that the use of musical elements, like chords and cadences, takes place in a historically situated musical system, the possibility of understanding and appreciating music presupposes familiarity with that system (LC 9:27, 9:39, 9:41; LA I:15). The rules of music are not fixed rule-formulations that would determine all and only correct applications thereof. Rather, the musical practices themselves sustain and transmit the rules that are given in the concrete applications thereof.

The rules of music are not regulative in that they would dictate what counts as acceptable or good music. Unlike traffic rules regulating driving that can be done without following those rules, the rules of music constitute the very domain of musical expression. Without a system, no expression, whether linguistic or musical, would have a role or function and hence no meaning to speak of. It would be "anything, or nothing" or, as Kant put it, "original nonsense" (PI §6, CPJ 5:308). Like the rules of grammar that allow us to express original thoughts in language and, for example, answer a given question in a number of different way, so too the rules of music open up a space of different expressive opportunities.

As an illustration of the scope of musical expression, Wittgenstein tells a history of Brahms, who rejected Josef Joachim's suggestion to change the beginning of his *Fourth Symphony*. Wittgenstein asks: "What reason could be given for rejecting it?," and offers what he sees as a viable answer:

> You misunderstand me: I know why you suggested that; you think this is what I meant to say, but it wasn't.
> It's not: this does not produce <u>feeling</u> I want to produce. (LC 9:30)

That Brahms's response is given in intentional terms (i.e., in terms of what he *meant* to say), should not lead us into thinking that the composer's intentions are independent of music. The possibility of expressing anything in music arises together with the musical system, and the musical intentions are *musical* from the beginning, not conceptual thoughts or emotions translated into the musical medium. Again, the operative thought pertains to the internal connection that Wittgenstein takes to obtain not just between the aesthetic judgment and its object but also between intentions and their expressions, whether linguistic or musical.

That music is constituted by rules does not entail that those rules determine the specific content of musical expressions or aesthetic judgments about music. In fact, it entails the exact opposite. This is because Wittgenstein's reason for underscoring the notion of a rule – both in philosophy of language and aesthetics – is intended as a guard against naturalistic explanations of meaning and understanding. If the aesthetic choices made by the composer in writing music, the musician in performing it, or the listener in judging it aesthetically reflected empirical regularities, then the aesthetic domain would be closer to a natural mechanism. But since aesthetic choices are made within a system of conventional rules, we can treat those choices as grounded in reasons and in that sense intentional rather than mechanistic. In other words, the sort of normativity that lies at the core of Wittgenstein's approach and is expressed by reference to the notion of a rule goes hand in hand with intentionality and hence freedom, at least when freedom is understood in the Kantian sense of responsiveness to reasons we give to ourselves (see Allison 1986; Allison 1990, 204–207). But this just means that the Kantian contrast between nature and freedom, which I argued to underpin Wittgenstein's early ethics, is still discernible in his middle period. Now the contrast emerges in Wittgenstein's distinction between the normatively laden beautiful over the causally induced agreeable and in his emphasis on reasons over causes in aesthetic explanations.

As indicated by the disagreement between Brahms and Joachim, Wittgenstein is open to the possibility of genuine aesthetic disagreements. Although the rules of an aesthetic system ground the possibility of aesthetic expression and aesthetic judgments, not all aesthetic disagreements can be resolved by appeal to rules. People disagree on the value of Mahler's music or Shakespeare's drama, prefer one way of stressing the rhythm of Klopstock's poetry over another, and make such fine-grained aesthetic judgments as "That doesn't look quite right yet" or "This bass ought to be quieter" (LC 9:19, 9:22; LA I:12).[35] The attempt to justify such judgments by reference to rule-formulations only takes us so far. To be sure, a teacher of counterpoint *can* correct a student's mistake in a voice-leading exercise by pointing out that her attempt does not conform to the rules of counterpoint as formulated in a harmony textbook. But it is unlikely that either Brahms's or Joachim's preferred opening for the *Fourth Symphony* includes a mistake in this sense. Both alternatives likely conform to the rules constitutive of Western romantic

---

[35] These examples relate to Wittgenstein's reflections on his own aesthetic judgments. On Wittgenstein's puzzlement with Shakespeare's high reputation, see Schulte 2013 and Huemer 2013; on his distaste of Mahler's music, see Guter 2015, 433–435.

music but aim at realizing different expressive possibilities that lie within the musical system. This implies that, in addition to the aesthetic system providing the necessary framework for aesthetic judgments, those judgments incorporate a personal element – a moment of endorsement, as it were, that reveals something about the musical thinking of its maker. As Wittgenstein says: "Every artist has been influenced by others & shows (the) traces of that influence in his works; but what we get from him is all the same only his own personality" (CV, 27 [23]).

For Wittgenstein, aesthetic discussions like the one between Brahms and Joachim may reveal "something which might be called a difference of taste: e.g., Yes, you always prefer slightly stronger contrasts, I always prefer slightly weaker" (LC 9:4). Importantly, such a "difference of taste needn't be as simple as 'I like this,' 'You like that,'" as it is in the case of the agreeableness of tastes and smells (LC 9:4). In explaining the personal aspect involved in aesthetic disagreements, Wittgenstein refers to aesthetic "ideals" (LC 9:18–22, 31–34).[36] This notion, just like the notion of an aesthetic "paradigm," functions as a placeholder for the standard against which aesthetic judgments are made and disagreements assessed. It is "like a norm of judgment," as Joachim Schulte notes (Schulte 2018, 227). Yet, Wittgenstein repeatedly states that it is impossible to pin down what that ideal or paradigm actually is without turning back to the aesthetic phenomenon itself (see LC 9:22; LA III:5; PI §537):

> And the idea suggests itself that there *must* be a paradigm somewhere in our mind, and that we have adjusted the tempo to conform to that paradigm. But in most cases if someone asked me "How do you think this melody should be played?" I will, as an answer, just whistle it in a particular way, and nothing will have been present to my mind but the tune *actually whistled* (not an image of *that*). (BBB, 166)

Getting closer to a given ideal takes place within an aesthetic system, which includes the different aesthetic alternatives as possible moves one can make: "to find what ideal we're directed to, you must look at what we do" (LC 9:22). Hence, aesthetic investigation is not unlike mathematical problem-solving. In 1941, Wittgenstein still writes:

> Take a theme like that of Haydn's (St. Antony Chorale), take the part of one of Brahms's variations corresponding to the first part of the theme, and set the task of constructing the second part of the variation in the style of the first part. That is a problem of the same kind as mathematical problems are. If the

---

[36] Aesthetic ideals may be culturally shared, like the "ideal of Greek Sculpture," but they may also be personal (LC 9:24). When Wittgenstein states that "my ideal is a certain coolness," he is not talking about shared cultural norms but articulating his own aesthetic preference, albeit one developed relation to the shared domain of the arts (CV, 4 [2]).

solution is found, say as Brahms gives it, then one has no doubt; – that is the solution.

We are agreed on this route. And yet, it is obvious here that there may easily be different routes, on each of which we can be in agreement, each of which we might call consistent. (RFM VII §11)

By connecting the personal ideals to the shared aesthetic system, Wittgenstein's account of aesthetic judgment overcomes both aesthetic object-ivism and subjectivism. In trying to get the accompaniment right, we are not "trying to discover a truth" that is out there independently of our own activity (LC 9:22). Aesthetic judgments do not rest on merely subjective feelings either, because the very development of aesthetic ideals requires a grasp of the possibilities available in the aesthetic system in question. Accordingly, there is room for aesthetic disagreements that are neither like disagreements on the agreeableness of tastes or smells nor like disagreements on statements about empirical reality.

The personal endorsement involved in an aesthetic judgment entails that justifications given by reference to rule-formulations do not exhaustively settle the case. Wittgenstein, keenly aware of this, gives the following example of an aesthetic explanation: "'Why is this note absolutely necessary?' Explanation would look like this: If you wrote out the tune in chords, you would see to which chord the note belongs. I.e. it hints at placing side by side with the tune a certain chorale" (LC 9:39). This sketch of an explanation of the note's necessity appeals to the rules of harmony and counterpoint. Resembling a basic exercise in chorale writing where one is asked to write a chord for each note of the melody, Wittgenstein's recommended course of action would reveal the role of the note within the hierarchical structure of the scale. One would notice, for example, that the note – the sixth of the scale, say – belongs to the subdominant chord and hence takes the melody to a point of relative stability before it moves on to the dominant or, alternatively, to the tonic.[37] But importantly, the ultimate force of the explanation resides in Wittgenstein's claim that, if you did this exercise, "you would see to which note the chord belongs" (LC 9:39). That is, you would *see* (or hear) the place of the note within the system. Moreover, you would see

---

[37] I deliberately talk about the scale (such as the major or the minor scale) rather than key (such as G major). In my view, Wittgenstein's musical examples are best understood in terms of the tonal functions of the different scale degrees. These functions remain the same regardless of the specific key in which the tune is written, as they reflect the overall shape of the scale that may be transposed to any given key. Hence, when Wittgenstein says that "you would see to which chord the note belongs," he is not talking about, for example, the C major chord. Instead, he is drawing attention to the harmonic function of the chord as, for example, the subdominant chord and thereby to the tonal function of the individual, "necessary" note. It is possible to hear that function, just as it is possible to hear whether the tune is in major or minor, without knowing the specific key in which the tune is performed.

(or hear) that, unlike some other notes that one could dispense without too much damage to the overall shape of the tune, the note in question fulfills a function without which the tune would be incomplete.

In Wittgenstein's early philosophy, seeing was the mode of grasping that aspect of language and reality which cannot be said. While we can express every imaginable fact in language, we cannot express the form that makes linguistic expression possible. Instead, we *see* the form directly in propositions of logic, mathematical equations, and – as I suggested – in musical themes. The same insight still informs Wittgenstein's discussion in 1933, even if the focus now is on aesthetic systems instead of an isolated tune resembling a tautology.[38] The moment of grasping the tonal function of the note within the scale, and hence grasping the tune as an "organized whole" to which the note belongs, is the moment where discursive justifications come to an end (LW1 §677). After the exercise of writing the tune in chords, I must rely on my ability to *see* the note's necessity. Likewise, if I try to justify my aesthetic judgment of the note's necessity to others, I must appeal to their ability to see it for themselves. And if, for some reason, you fail to *see* the note's necessity and thus disagree with my judgment, no rule-formulation will be sufficient to convince you. In aesthetics, "A solution must speak for itself. If when I've made you see what I see, it doesn't appeal to you, there is an end" (LC 9:31).

### 3.4 The Objective and the Subjective Moments of Aesthetic Judgment

Aesthetic systems are shared, historically transmitted, and normatively struc-tured practices. In addition to the grammatical relations between the elements of the systems, the normativity carries over to our aesthetic judgments, which employ notions of correctness, rightness, and wrongness. We also hold those making aesthetic judgments countable. We expect reasons for their judgments and "distinguish between a person who knows what he is talking about and a person who doesn't" (LA I:17). The arts in particular rest on convention and the sort of communal agreement that Wittgenstein takes to be essential for language (PI §§242, 355).

In the 1938 lectures on aesthetics, the contrast between the beautiful and the agreeable as kinds of judgments recedes to the background, giving way to the equally Kantian contrast between reasons and causes as modes of explanation (see G 4:412; CPJ 5:387). Wittgenstein claims that in real life "aesthetic

---

[38] Here, I disagree with Peter Hacker, according to whom the later Wittgenstein abandons his early distinction between saying and showing, treats ethics and religion "naturalistically or anthropo-logically as forms of life," and presumes that "there is nothing ineffable about ethics, aesthetics and religion" (Hacker 2001, 39).

adjectives such as 'beautiful,' 'fine,' etc., play hardly any role at all" and repeats the view that the word "beautiful" is all too easily misunderstood as a name of a property (LA I:8,1; see LC 9:19). In spite of this heightened caution about the term, the main insight motivating Wittgenstein's earlier contrast between the beautiful and the agreeable continues to dominate his discussion.[39] He still states: "I see roughly this – there is a realm of utterance of delight, when you taste pleasant food or smell a pleasant smell, etc., then there is the realm of Art which is quite different, though often you may make the same face when you hear a piece of music as when you taste good food" (LA II:3). The two types of judgments pertaining to sensibility are sharply contrasted despite the overlap in their manifest expressions. Moreover, the key difference still resides in the accountability of the judging subject, whose reasons for the judgment ought to be relevantly related to the judgment and transparent to the subject. Connecting aesthetic accountability to intentional action, Wittgenstein notes: "In a law-court you are asked the motive of your action and you are supposed to know it.... You are not supposed to know the laws by which your body and mind are governed" (LA III:12; see LC 9:32; PI II §262). To know one's motives does not require introspective access to the contents of one's mind. Rather, just as grammar grounds the internal connections between motive and action, desire and its fulfillment, or fear and its intentional object, aesthetic reasons arise within the context to which the judgment belongs.

Given that aesthetic systems are autonomous and cannot be explained by reference to another domain, the relevant kinds of reasons "are in the nature of further descriptions" (LC 9:31). Sometimes, the explanations take the form of comparisons between the aesthetic object and something else. One may find an object of comparison from dance, gestures, facial expressions, or the realm of language as when comparing a musical phrase to a conclusion, question, or an answer (LC 9:31; LA III:1; BBB, 166; CV, 79–81 [69–70]). Sometimes the explanations aim at placing an artwork in its cultural context by connecting it to other works by the same artist or by comparing it with the works of someone else. For example, "by making a person hear lots of different pieces by Brahms, you can make him see what he's driving at" (LC 9:31). Even explanations given by reference to rule-formulations, like Wittgenstein's own explanation of the similarity of musical works by Palestrina and Brahms, namely, that "they start from tonic, go to dominant, & return to tonic," could be understood as descriptions rather than explanations in the scientific sense, because what is explained

---

[39] Before the 2016 publication of Moore's full notes from 1933, the notes from 1938 were the main source on Wittgenstein's aesthetics. This contributed, for example, to the mistaken view that Wittgenstein rejected the notion of the beautiful altogether and hence took Kant's aesthetics to rest on a misunderstanding (see Lewis 1998, 21).

is not subsumed under an independently established law or principle but simply characterized in terms of the tonal functions manifest in and upheld by the works themselves (LC 9:33). In each case, the aesthetic "explanation" aims at directing attention to the object of aesthetic appreciation within its context. In this respect, Wittgenstein claims, aesthetic investigation is similar to grammatical investigation (LA II:17–18, 38; III:12; LC 9:32).

That the arts and crafts are historically developing and culturally variable phenomena means that the mastery of any given field requires initiation into its conventions by practice and drilling. It also means that, once initiated, individuals can make a mark on those practices, at least within certain boundaries. In comparison to the romantic idea of a genius who creates *ex nihilo* guided by nothing but inspiration, Wittgenstein's stance on artistic creativity is cautious, even conservative.[40] According to him, "all the greatest composers wrote in accordance with [the rules of harmony]" (LA I:16). When someone in class objects to the view, probably appealing to creativity and originality as essential features of art, Wittgenstein responds: "You can say that every composer changed the rules, but the variation was very slight; not all the rules were changed. The music was still good by a great many of the old rules" (LA I:16). Given Wittgenstein's rule-based conception of language and his alignment of grammatical and aesthetic systems, it is important for him to emphasize the gradual and slow change of musical rules. This is because only a relatively stable musical system is capable of supporting the communal agreement in the rules that allows for meaningful artistic expression and for the possibility of understanding it (see PI §§199, 240–242).

At the same time, the conservatism of Wittgenstein's position should not be exaggerated. His conception of rules is flexible enough to accommodate a great variety of artistic styles and has resources to explain the kinds of changes that are often treated as evidence of the arts' inherent creativity. Yet, as the motto of the *Investigations* underscores, progress often looks greater than it really is (PI, 2). This is especially true when originality is treated as a supreme value and hence underscored at the expense of tradition, as it often is in the art world and theory of art. When Wagner or Schoenberg transform the musical vocabulary of the Western tradition and do so in ways often regarded as revolutionary, they do not begin from scratch, as John Cage perhaps did in "composing" his *4'33*. Wagner's and Schoenberg's music may still be understood and appreciated against the background of what came before. That some shared background is necessary for the possibility of understanding is evident in Wittgenstein's

---

[40] On Wittgenstein's relation to conservatism in general, see, for example, Nyiri 1982 and Janik 1989, 40–58.

remarks on modal music. Its difference from later Western music is vast enough to prevent understanding; yet, pointing to similarities between the modal and modern keys may help one understand the former (LC 9:41; PI §535; RPP1 §639).

Another measure against an overly conservative conception of the arts emerges in Wittgenstein's remarks on artistic masterpieces and the notion of a genius. According to him, we do not apply the terminology of correctness to Beethoven's music or Gothic Cathedrals, because these aesthetic phenomena strike us as "tremendous" or "grand."[41] For Wittgenstein, Mozart and Beethoven are the "actual sons of God," and he does not shy away from passing judgment on other composers (and thinkers) for their lack of genius (CC, 19). Yet, in contrast with most romantic aestheticians, who took freedom from conventions to be the essential mark of the genius, Wittgenstein has a more balanced view of the relation between conventions and originality in art. Distinguishing between character and talent, he claims that while those we call genius have both, the role of character in them is more dominant: "Genius is not 'talent and character,' but character manifesting itself in the form of a special talent" (CV, 40 [35]; see CV, 41, 49–50, 75 [43, 65]).

One can find echoes of Schopenhauer's as well as Otto Weininger's ideas in Wittgenstein's notion of genius (cf. Weininger 1906, 103–113; Schopenhauer 1969, 184–195). Especially Schopenhauer was influenced by Kant, and Kant's conception of the works of genius (if not exactly his notion of genius itself) carries over to Wittgenstein's remarks. This is especially true regarding the balance that both seek to find between artistic conventions and originality. For Kant, the genius provides original sensuous material for art, but that material must be cultivated by taste, which is "the discipline (or corrective) of genius, clipping its wings and making it well behaved or polished" (CPJ 5:319; see 5:310). This is because if the artist did not adhere to the rules of artistic practices, his works would be unintelligible to others (CPJ 5:307–308). This idea may be seen as prefiguring Wittgenstein's later argument about communally shared rules grounding the possibility of communication (PI §§240–242).[42]

So when introduced to a given aesthetic field, be that poetry, tailoring, or music, one must learn the rules constitutive of the practice. The possibility of making and refining aesthetic judgments arises only via such immersion into our shared form of life. At the same time, aesthetic judgments involve an irreducibly subjective moment of seeing for oneself. Kant argued that there

---

[41] On the "tremendous things in art," see Schulte 1989; Tilghman 1991, 86–87; Lewis 1996; Tam 2002.

[42] On Kant and Wittgenstein on genius, see Lewis 2005.

cannot be objective (i.e., conceptually determinable), rules of taste that we could apply to determine what is beautiful. Nor can we make pure judgments of taste by imitating others. Taste requires that one can judge the model itself and do so by relying on one's own feeling (CPJ 5:231–232). In the same vein, while emphasizing familiarity with conventional, shared rules of art as a prerequisite of aesthetic judgment, Wittgenstein denies the possibility of discursively establishing the validity aesthetic judgments. Like Kant, he refers to *feeling* as a central component of aesthetic judgment, mentioning "seeing" and "feeling" as "verbs describing personal experience" relevant for aesthetic judgments (LA I:3; see BBB, 48; CV, 83–84 [73]).

In the *Brown Book*, dictated in 1934–5, Wittgenstein examines a series of examples of experiences of sensuous phenomena. One is that of being impressed by a particular way of reading a sentence:

> I have read a line with a peculiar attention; I am impressed by the reading, and this makes me say that I have observed something besides the mere seeing of the written signs and the speaking of words. I have also expressed it by saying that I have noticed a particular atmosphere round the seeing and speaking. (BBB, 177)

What the peculiar attention with which the line is read brings to focus is not the words themselves or the propositional content they express. What is brought to focus instead is the "atmosphere" round the sentence. Another metaphor he uses is facial features. As noted, the metaphor of facial features appears already in the *Tractatus* as an illustration of internal properties that *show* themselves but cannot be said (TLP 4.1221). I do not think it is a coincidence that Wittgenstein concludes his remarks on the experience of reading by reference to the *Tractatus*'s distinction between saying and showing. When read with that peculiar attention, "the sentence has shown me something, ... I have noticed something in it" (BBB, 178). What I notice does not render itself to a discursive explanation, but depends on turning my attention away from the discursive content to the aesthetic "surface" of the sentence.

Wittgenstein aligns the case of reading with other examples drawn from the aesthetic domain broadly construed. He mentions observing the lighting of a room, being impressed by the color patterns of flowers, and listening to a piece of music (BBB, 175, 178). In such cases, he says, we are tempted to ask what it is that these phenomena convey. However, looking for a determinate answer is in vain, for what we are impressed by lies in the sensuous features or patterns of the phenomenon. According to him, "We wish to avoid any form of expression which would seem to refer to an effect produced by an object on a subject. (Here we are bordering on the problem of idealism and realism and on the problem whether statements of aesthetics are subjective or objective)" (BBB, 178). Here, I take idealism to be the view according to which the beauty of an aesthetic phenomenon, say, rests solely on personal experience, whereas realism is the view according to which beauty resides in the properties of the object. These positions naturally go hand in hand with subjectivism and objectivism about aesthetic judgments. For subjectivists, the judgment is *"merely subjective, a matter of taste"* (BBB, 48). For objectivists, the judgment is about the object itself and either true or false. I have argued that, while Wittgenstein rejects the sort of subjectivism that takes aesthetic judgments to be *merely* subjective, he does not fall back on aesthetic objectivism. For him, just as for Kant, aesthetic judgments include both an objective and a subjective component. This, in turn, points to a possible way of overcoming both dogmatic idealism and dogmatic realism – just as it does for Kant.

In 1938, Wittgenstein describes the interplay between the conventional, objective side and the subjective side of aesthetic judgments as the development of taste:

> In the case of the word "correct" you have a variety of related cases. There is first the case in which you learn the rules. The cutter learns how long a coat is to be, how wide the sleeve must be, etc. He learns the rules – he is drilled – as in music you are drilled in harmony and counterpoint. Suppose I went in for tailoring and I first learnt all the rules, I might have, on the whole, two sorts of attitude. (1) Lewy says: "This is too short." I say: "No. It is right. It is according to the rules." (2) I develop a feeling for the rules. I interpret the rules. I might say: "No. It isn't right. It isn't according to the rules." Here I would be making an aesthetic judgment about the thing which is according to the rules in sense (1). On the other hand, if I hadn't learnt the rules, I wouldn't be able to make the aesthetic judgment. In learning the rules you get a more and more refined judgment. Learning the rules actually changes your judgment. (LA I:15)

The first stage of aesthetic development is an immersion into the conventions of a given field, resembling Wittgenstein's mature account of the learning of language (see, e.g., PI §§143–184). I am drilled in the rules constitutive of the game and learn to discriminate between correct and incorrect moves in that game. However, even if we could explain artistic creativity by appeal to the constitutive character of the rules, possible differences in taste are not accounted for by rules only, as the disagreement between Brahms and Joachim shows. Hence, Wittgenstein claims, in the second stage of my aesthetic development, I "develop a feeling for the rules" (LA I:15). In taking a stance on the rules themselves, in "interpreting" the rules, and in disagreeing with a basically correct but for me aesthetically dissatisfying solution, I am first and foremost relying on my personal, subjectively felt experience of the phenomenon in question (LA I:15,17).

The importance that Wittgenstein assigns to the subjective side of aesthetic judgment is evident in his statement: "Perhaps the most important thing in connection with aesthetics is what may be called aesthetic reactions, e.g. discontent, disgust, discomfort" (LA II:10).[43] Such aesthetic reactions are personal responses to particular aesthetic phenomena, evoked in relation to what Wittgenstein calls aesthetic puzzles. His examples of such puzzles include the design of a door in an architectural context and a musical performance that is not quite satisfying from the viewer's or listener's perspective. The puzzles concern the possibility of mending the object so that it meets the viewer's or listener's aesthetic ideal: perhaps the door should be higher or the bass line in the musical performance stronger. In contrast to Kant and a number of other aestheticians who emphasize pleasure derived from the arts and other objects of aesthetic appreciation like nature as a sine qua non of aesthetic experience, Wittgenstein highlights negative responses.[44] Unlike the state of equilibrium I may experience when listening to a perfectly balanced musical performance, aesthetic dissatisfaction or puzzlement forces me to look for a solution, thereby making me fully aware of the aesthetic puzzle and the call to judge the phenomenon aesthetically.

Another kind of aesthetic puzzle is exemplified by Wittgenstein's repeated quest for finding the right object of comparison for a musical theme or a phrase. Even if there is no aesthetic flaw in the theme, one may still feel a puzzlement: "One asks such a question as 'What does this remind me of?' or one says of a piece of music: 'This is like some sentence, but what sentence is it like?'" (LA III:1). When an apt object of comparison is found, one experiences a "click": all of a sudden the theme, seen in light of the comparison, makes sense (LA III:1). A similar "click" of aesthetic satisfaction arises when a disturbing feature is amended by finding the right rhythm, tempo, or accentuation for a performance – when the aesthetic object is as it "should" be (LA II:9–10). Yet, Wittgenstein notes,

What does it mean to say 'It's right'? Can I prove to anyone that it is?

> You might say it means: I'm now satisfied; I'm in a state of equilibrium, not of tension.
>
> This may be a good metaphor, but there isn't <u>one</u> feeling which characterizes the thousand different cases of equilibrium. (LC 9:30–31)

---

[43] On Wittgenstein's notion of aesthetic reactions, see, for example, Lewis 1998; Säätelä 2002; Tam 2002.

[44] One should not forget that Kant, too, mentions displeasure as an equally relevant response to an aesthetically contemplated form (see CPJ FI 20:224).

Why should we care about the subjective side aesthetic judgment? Why does Wittgenstein claim that the aesthetic reactions of discontent, disgust, or discomfort are perhaps the most important thing about aesthetics? And why does he repeatedly bring up personal experiences such as the "click" or "equilibrium" of aesthetic satisfaction as central for aesthetic investigation, elsewhere compared to grammatical investigation? Is not such a personal experience just a "wheel that can be turned though nothing else moves with it" or a "beetle" in a box that "doesn't belong to the language game at all; not even as a *Something*" (PI §§271, 293; see Makkai 2021, 56)? In Section 4.2, I will return to this question and argue that this is not the case.

## 4 From the *Brown Book* to the *Philosophical Investigations*

### 4.1 Form and Content

A central question in aesthetics concerns the meaning and the understanding of art. Traditional answers to these closely related questions resemble those given in philosophy of language. Throughout the history of aesthetics, we find representational theories of artistic meaning, such as Plato's view of art as the imitation of appearances; expression theories, such as Collingwood's account of art as the expression of the artist's intentions; and arousal theories that treat the feelings aroused by art in the audience as art's content. The latter two are sometimes, as in Tolstoy's *What is Art?*, combined. The artist's intention, which, especially in the Romantic era, was taken to be emotive, gives rise to a work of art. The work itself is an external sign designed for the purpose of communicating that intention. The audience, in turn, is supposed to grasp the work's content by interpreting the artist's intention based on the work's properties.

In each case, the meaning of the artwork resides somewhere beyond the work itself, whether in the represented reality or in the private mind of the artist. To understand the work, the audience must either grasp the represented or expressed content or find themselves in an emotive state that matches the one expressed, intended, or imitated by the work. Especially representational theories give rise to the additional question of truth: If the work has cognitive content, we may ask how faithfully that content matches reality and hence whether the work is capable of giving us knowledge about the world. We may also ask whether the represented, expressed, or aroused content, whether emotional or other, is beneficial or morally worthy. Such considerations led Plato and Tolstoy to recommend censorship, as they took certain emotions to be harmful for the audience and for the society as a whole.

Kantians and other formalists have been apprehensive about the traditional theories, because those theories seem to assign a subservient role to the specifically artistic and aesthetic features of art, thereby undermining art's autonomy. For them, it is a mistake to assimilate the reception of the arts to the discursive model of propositional knowledge. Art should be treated as an end in itself, and the highest gains of art are taken to depend on art's specifically artistic, formal, or sensuous features. Nevertheless, Kant himself argues that pure judgments of taste can contribute to cognition, but only and precisely in virtue of being nonconceptual (CPJ 5:217, 5:287). That the formal features of art are capable of revealing something essential about reality appears repeatedly in subsequent German philosophy. Friedrich Schleiermacher, Schopenhauer, Friedrich Schelling, Friedrich Nietzsche, Hans-Georg Gadamer, Theodor Adorno, as well as the Austrian formalist Eduard Hanslick all imply, in their respective ways, that art and especially music discloses something essential about the world by its specifically artistic forms.

The notion of art's extra-artistic content, which motivates the traditional theories of artistic meaning and is still discussed by aestheticians, albeit in a more specialized and fine-grained fashion, fits awkwardly with Wittgenstein's commitment to aesthetic autonomy. It is thus no surprise that he is critical of each of the traditional accounts. Commenting on Tolstoy's *What is Art?*, he writes:

> There is *much* that could be learned from Tolstoy's false theorizing that the work of art conveys "a feeling." – And you really might call it, if not the expression of a feeling, an expression of feeling, or a felt expression. And you might say too that people who understand it to that extent "resonate" with it, respond to it. You might say: The work of art does not seek to convey *something else*, just itself.…
>
> And it does start to be really absurd, to say, the artist wishes that, what he feels when writing, the other should feel when reading. Presumably I can think I understand a poem (e.g.), understand it in the way its author would wish, – but what *he* may have felt in writing it, that doesn't concern me *at all*. (CV, 67 [58–59])

The absurdity of treating the artist's private feelings as the content of their art lies in the fact that the two are only externally related to one another. We do speak about understanding a poem as its author intended, but just as "it is only in a language that I can mean something by something," artistic intentions are not independent of the medium of their expression (PI, 22, see PI §§243–248). As explained above, for Wittgenstein, the musician's intentions, thoughts, and ideas are *musical* from the very beginning, related to music as the meaning of "If it doesn't rain, I shall go for walk" relates to the sentence (PI, 22; see PPF

§§35–51 [PI, vi]; LW1 §§373–382).[45] Insofar as the intention is not captured by its expression, it drops out of the picture as superfluous.

Wittgenstein's remarks on the arousal theory similarly target the contingency of the link between the work and aroused feelings:

> It has sometimes been said that what music conveys to us are feelings of joyfulness, melancholy, triumph, etc, etc. and what repels us in this account is that it seems to say that music is an instrument for producing in us sequences of feelings. And from this one might gather that any other means of producing such feelings would do for us instead of music. – To such an account we are tempted to reply "Music conveys to us *itself*!" (BBB, 178)

Like his criticism of confusing the beautiful with the agreeable, Wittgenstein's stance on the arousal theory has an almost ethical undertone. The failure to appreciate art for its own sake in favor of merely subjective sensuous effects is to subsume art to a mechanistic, causal model. If art is treated as a mere instrument of producing effects – which is of course possible – then it becomes redundant. Such effects could equally well be drawn from other resources. The same argument may be extended to aesthetic cognitivism, according to which art has both the ability and the purpose to provide propositional knowledge about the world. While ostensibly nobler than sensuous pleasure or emotional rush, potential cognitive gains of art could also be acquired by other and probably more efficient means.

Wittgenstein's arguments against the expression and arousal theories accord with his later account of language, which similarly attacks the explanation of meaning by reference to the mental acts, states, processes, or dispositions of the speaker or the listener (e.g., BBB, 21–22, 64; PR §§12–22; PI §§143–184, 437–440). Wittgenstein is usually credited for questioning the relevance of mental states for the constitution of meaning, but similar views can be found in the history of aesthetics. The alignment of artistic intentions and their expressions figures in Kant's emphasis on the communicability of art and his characterization of the artist's "aesthetic ideas" as sensible representations of the imagination which "no language fully attains or can make intelligible" (CPJ 5:314; see CPJ 5:307–308). The point is formulated even more sharply by Hanslick, who rejects the expression theory of music by arguing that whatever "does not become outwardly apparent is, so far as music is concerned, altogether nonexistent, but whatever has become apparent has ceased to be mere intention" (Hanslick 1986, 36).

---

[45] I use the 2009 edition of the *Philosophical Investigations* throughout this book. References to "Philosophy of Psychology: A Fragment" (PPF), which used to be known as Part II of *Philosophical Investigations*, are cited from both the 2009 and 1958 editions. References to the latter are given in square brackets.

The dismissal of the causal model of art's reception is equally typical in the Kantian tradition. Kant notes that if empirically conditioned pleasure "were all that is at stake, then it would be foolish to be scrupulous with regard to the means for providing ourselves with it" (CPJ 5:208). Wittgenstein makes the same observation: "If we have a certain arrangement of colours & say it is beautiful, & you suggest that what this means is that it gives us pleasure. I ask: Why should we use so many different means to get pleasure?" (LC 9:18–19). Hanslick reprimands listeners who voluntarily subject themselves to music's empirically conditioned effects and as a result ignore the specifically musical. Such listeners treat musical works like "products of nature," on a par with a fine cigar or a spicy delicacy, and could equally well resort to using sulfuric ether and chloroform (Hanslick 1986, 60; see BBB, 178; LC 9:20; LA II:2–3). Even animals are influenced by music, but we do not treat their reactions as signs of aesthetic understanding (Hanslick 1986, 61–62; see CPJ 5:210). Wittgenstein uses the same illustrations. Juxtaposing art with nature, he notes that to seek emotional effects from music is to treat music as a drug (BBB, 178). And he distinguishes the understanding of music from its causal effects by reference to animals: "We use the phrase 'A man is musical' not so as to call a man musical if he says 'Ah!' when a piece of music is played, any more than we call a dog musical if it wags its tail when music is played" (LA I:17).

It has been argued that Wittgenstein's reasons for rejecting the expression and arousal theories are exhausted by his rejection of reductionism and his anti-Cartesian "anxiety" and that he should be open to other explanations of art's extra-artistic content.[46] It has also been argued, originally by appealing to the *Tractatus*'s idea of structural isomorphism between propositions and facts, that the resemblances between music and emotions serve to ground the expressive content of music (see Langer 1942, 221–245). The argument is not successful by the *Tractatus*'s lights, as it overlooks the requirement of referential relations between names and objects for the determinacy of sense (TLP 2.1513–2.1515). Nor does it fit with the position of the later Wittgenstein, who adamantly denies the conclusion. As late as in 1948, he writes:

> Understanding & explaining a musical phrase. – The simplest explanation is sometimes a gesture; another might be a dance step, or words describing a dance. – But isn't our understanding of the phrase an experience we have while hearing it? & what function, in that case, has the explanation? Are we supposed to think of *it* while we hear music? Are we supposed to imagine the dance, or whatever it may be, as we listen? And supposing we do, – why should *that* be called hearing the music with understanding?? If seeing the

---

[46] For proposals on how Wittgenstein's later view could be combined with art's emotive content, see Scruton 2004 and Hagberg 1995, 99–109.

dance is what matters, it would be better *that*, rather than the music, were performed. But that is all a misunderstanding. (CV, 79 [69])

This reduction, once again, gives the musical phrase a sovereign identity by insisting that the content of music cannot be translated into another medium without loss. Even if music resembles other phenomena, like gestures, facial expressions, or dance steps, such resemblances do not warrant the ascription of extramusical content to musical phrases or themes.[47]

That the content of music cannot be expressed in another medium without loss is the core thesis of musical formalism. Hanslick, the main proponent of the view, argues that while music resembles the dynamic of human emotions, it does not have any specific extramusical subject matter. Instead, "the content of music is tonally moving forms" (Hanslick 1986, 29). Hence, the use of emotive terminology in our descriptions of music should not be read literally (30). A similar view follows from Wittgenstein's later conception of language.[48] If the meaning of words and sentences is their use within a linguistic context, then, mutatis mutandis, musical notes, chords, cadences, and tunes acquire their meaning from the role they have within the musical system. This is why it is impossible to translate them it into pictures or words. For the same reason, in order to explain the content of music, I can either describe the roles of the musical elements within the system ("This is the dominant," etc.), resort to indirect descriptions or comparisons that aim at illuminating the musical phrase, or else just whistle the tune.

In Section 3.2, I noted that just as the content of fear is partly constituted by its intentional object, aesthetic judgments are internally related or "directed" to the object of aesthetic appreciation (LA II:18). In the *Brown Book*, Wittgenstein refines the picture by making a move similar to his early shift from the comparison between a musical theme and a proposition to the comparison between the theme and a tautology (NB, 40). He introduces the idea of fear without any specific object of fear and calls such a feeling "intransitive" (BBB, 22). We may also talk about transitive and intransitive uses of words and sentences. The former warrants the question "What did you mean by that sentence?" to be answered by a discursive explanation or a paraphrase of the sentence, whilst the latter does not. In the intransitive case, the question is

---

[47] Oswald Hanfling aptly describes the experience as a "hearing-as-if" experience (Hanfling 2004, 152).

[48] Here, I disagree with Allan Janik and Stephen Toulmin who call Hanslick the "voice of mediocrity" (Janik and Toulmin 1973, 35) and with Béla Szabados who contrasts Wittgenstein's later account of music with Hanslick's formalism (Szabados 2014, 59–72, 87–97). On my reading, the similarities between the two Viennese greats surpass the differences and reflect their shared background in the Kantian tradition (see Appelqvist 2019a).

rather: "What sentence is formed by this sequence of words?" (BBB, 161). At this point, it should be no surprise that the phenomena Wittgenstein mentions to exemplify intransitive meaning are from the aesthetic domain broadly conceived:

> The same strange illusion which we are under when we seem to seek something which a face expresses whereas, in reality, we are giving ourselves up to the features before us – that same illusion possesses us even more strongly if repeating a tune to ourselves and letting it make its full impression on us, we say "This tune says *something*," and it is as though I had to find *what* it says. And yet I know that it doesn't say anything such that I might express in words or pictures what it says. And if, recognizing this, I resign myself to saying "It just expresses a musical thought," this would mean no more that saying "It expresses itself." (BBB, 166)

Since intransitive meaning resides in the structure of the sentence, in the exact choice of its words and their order, it cannot be explained by any other means except by repeating the sentence – a feature of language that Wittgenstein in 1931 connects with "the Kantian solution of the problem of philosophy" (CV, 13 [10]). Intransitive meaning thus has a role analogous to Wittgenstein's early logical form, whose inexpressibility he illustrated by reference to facial features and music (TLP 4.014, 4.1221).[49]

Art's autonomy and the inadequacy of our discursive resources for explaining the content of art are common commitments among Kantians and other formalists. What is less common, though, is the extension of the idea to language, typically treated as a means of communicating extralinguistic facts. While the later Wittgenstein is famous for emphasizing the *uses* of language, he is also highly sensitive to the specifically linguistic, formal features of language. In his early view, the *form* of language, which is independent of empirical content, is the necessary condition for the possibility of sense. In his later period, while dismissing the formal unity of language envisioned in the *Tractatus*, Wittgenstein still talks about language as a "family of structures" (PI §108). He calls such structures "language-games" – a notion which becomes more prominent from 1932 onward and eventually replaces that of a grammatical system (see LC 7:21, 7:92–95; BBB, 81; PI §§7, 23–24). And for Wittgenstein, grammar is autonomous: "the rules of grammar may be called 'arbitrary,' if that is to mean that the *purpose* of grammar is nothing but that of language" (PI §497). What makes Wittgenstein's inquiry grammatical is that the inquiry is not directed toward empirical

---

[49] For discussions on intransitive meaning and aesthetics, see Johannessen 1990; Hagberg 1995, 99–117; Escalera 2012.

phenomena, but toward the *possibilities* of phenomena, those possibilities being grounded in grammar (PI §§89–90; cf. TLP 2.0121).

A commitment to aesthetic autonomy does not mean that one takes art to be isolated from other aspects of the human form of life, any more than grammar is detached from practical purposes and endeavors. But the nature of that relation calls for a more delicate analysis than the traditional accounts of art afford. I take it to be undeniable that the specifically artistic forms of different aesthetic systems have a central place in Wittgenstein's conception of aesthetics. But he also points out, especially in 1938 and after, that the investigation into aesthetics does not begin "from certain words, but from certain occasions or activities" (LA I:6). In order to describe what aesthetic appreciation consists in, "we would have to describe the whole environment," "culture," or "ways of living" (LA I:20, 25, 35). According to him,

> What belongs to a language game is a whole culture. In describing musical taste you have to describe whether children give concerts, whether women do or whether men only give them, etc., etc. In aristocratic circles in Vienna people had [such and such] a taste, then it came into bourgeois circles and women joined choirs, etc. This is an example of tradition in music. (LA I:26)

It is hard to see how the observation of women joining choirs in a bourgeois society could serve as a solution to the kinds of puzzles Wittgenstein himself describes as central to aesthetics. So what is the role of such observations in Wittgenstein's overall understanding of aesthetics and the arts? What is it in his mature philosophy of language?

The word "language-game" is meant to underscore that the speaking of language belongs to an activity. But this does not mean that we could reductively explain language by reference to language-independent uses or purposes (PI §§23, 496; see PI II §365). The activities, customs, institutions, and our biological and social constitution, which together make up our human form of life, are irreducibly intertwined with language from the beginning. The objects we encounter, the thoughts we entertain, and the actions we perform are all shaped by grammar. Besides, keeping in mind the differences across the family of language-games, including artistic ways of using language, we should not assume that in each case we will find the sort of use that is characteristic of factual statements. As Wittgenstein reminds us: "Do not forget that a poem, even though it is composed in the language of information, is not used in the language-game of giving information" (Z §160). Considering such creative and artistic uses of language as making up stories, acting in a play, guessing riddles, cracking jokes, solving arithmetic problems, cursing, or praying – all examples featured in Wittgenstein's famous list of language-games – gives an idea of the expressive range that language actually has (see PI §23).

The sort of dichotomy between art and reality that typically underlies the traditional accounts of art and is presupposed by aesthetic cognitivism reflects an inflated emphasis on one function of language, namely, the communication of information. Moreover, it rests on a failure to acknowledge that whatever we call reality is already shaped by our forms of expression and thus belongs to the scope of language as understood by the later Wittgenstein. A similar embeddedness in our form of life shaped by language characterizes the arts. Instead of being translatable into words and sentences, music "interacts" with our language: "Does the theme point to nothing beyond itself? Oh yes! But that means: – The impression it makes on me is connected with things in its surroundings – e.g.: with the existence of the German language & of its intonation, but that means with the whole field of our language games" (CV, 59 [51–52]). Musical phrases resemble conclusions, questions, and answers. The musician's phrasing of a melody may accord with the intonation of a given language. And the performance of a string quartet is like a conversation between different voices. The works of a given composer are musically related to those of other composers, but they are also related to other fields of art like literature, poetry, or painting of the same period. And attentive listening to a musical performance and the listeners' understanding of the movement therein may be shown in their accompanying gestures or facial expressions of surprise, disgust, or delight.[50]

But it just does not follow from such connections and resemblances between music and something else that this "*something else*" gets closer to the content of music than what we hear in music itself (CV, 67 [58].). Besides, there is no reason to think that specifically artistic forms of expression could not be part of our expressive resources on their own terms: "If a theme, a phrase, suddenly means something to you, you don't have to be able to explain it. Just *this* gesture has been made accessible to you" (Z §158).

## 4.2 Meaning and Understanding

Wittgenstein compares language with music throughout his career, and the questions of meaning and understanding lie at the heart of the comparison. In 1915, he aligns musical tunes with tautologies and claims that "knowledge of the nature of logic will for this reason lead to knowledge of the nature of music" (NB, 40). The comparison between musical tunes and sentences surfaces again in the 1930s. Despite the changes in Wittgenstein's conception of language, the

---

[50] On such interconnections, see, for example, Schulte 1993, 37–44; Guter 2017.

point of the comparison still lies in the ineffability of the tune's meaning (LC 8:66). Moreover, the linguistic objects of comparison for music are still formal in character: a feature of a melody may be explained by comparing it with a colon or by characterizing a musical phrase as an answer to what came before (BBB, 166). However, in the *Brown Book*, the direction of the analogy between language and music has reversed. When the 1915 remark promises that knowledge of logic will shed light on music, Wittgenstein now states:

> What we call "understanding a sentence" has, in many cases, a much greater similarity to understanding a musical theme than we might be inclined to think. But I don't mean that understanding a musical theme is more like the picture which one tends to make oneself of understanding a sentence; but rather that this picture is wrong, and that understanding a sentence is much more like what really happens when we understand a tune than at first sight appears. For understanding a sentence, we say, points to a reality outside the sentence. Whereas one might say "Understanding a sentence means getting hold of its content; and the content of the sentence is *in* the sentence." (BBB, 167)

What is remarkable about this statement, which later appears slightly reformulated in the *Investigations*, is the suggestion that a proper grasp of *musical* understanding will illuminate the key theme of Wittgenstein's later philosophy, the understanding of language (see PI §527).

In the *Investigations*, the question of understanding is formulated as a question of following a rule. If linguistic meaning is best treated as the rule-governed use of a word or a sentence within the context of a language-game, then under what criteria am I entitled to say that I understand that meaning (PI §43)? It is not sufficient that my behavior conforms to the rule that is constitutive of the game providing the context of the use. If I understand, then my behavior ought to be internally related to the rule so that I can appeal to the rule in explaining my application thereof. The rule is, as the traditional interpretation notes, "involved in [my] activity as a reason or part of a reason for acting thus-and-so" (Baker and Hacker 2009, 138). Otherwise it would make no sense to talk about understanding, which is a normative notion standing in need of a criterion to distinguish it from misunderstanding.

Setting aside the seeming dissimilarity between the outwardly passive music listener and the speaker of language, the way in which the rule-following problem is formulated closely resembles the case of aesthetic judgments and their justification, discussed in Section 3.3.[51] On what grounds am I entitled to

---

[51] As indicated by his example of whistling a theme as an answer to the question of how it should be played, Wittgenstein's own take on the understanding of art includes a performative aspect (see BBB, 166; LC I:12; CV, 80 [70]; PI II §178; Hanfling 2004, 157–160).

say that I understand a musical phrase? A mere exclamation of pleasure is not enough to show that I understand because, as we have seen, pleasure may be only contingently related to music (LA I:17). Nor is it enough that I simply imitate the judgments of others by repeating the opinions of established experts and art critics. We do not attribute musical understanding to others unless we hear reasons for their judgments. We also expect those reasons to be relevantly related to music and transparent to the maker of the judgment, as Wittgenstein's analogy between an aesthetic discussion and a court-of-law illustrates (LC 9:32; LA III:12).

The rule-following discussion of the *Investigations* presents similar requirements for the understanding of language. If the question about my ability to follow a rule is "not a question about causes, then it is about the justification for my acting in *this* way in complying with the rule" (PI §217). And up to a point I *can* offer justifications. If I use an unusual word in conversation and someone asks what I mean, I can define the word. And I can explain the definition by substituting alternative expressions for the original ones. These are legitimate justifications for my use of the word, exhibiting my mastery of the grammar of the word. Moreover, they are – or so I argue – similar in kind to an explanation I give of Brahms's "wobbly" syncopated rhythm when I point out that the rhythm is 3 against 4 (LA III:10).

However, what I have accomplished by such justifications is new formulations of the original rule, whose application similarly stands in need of justification. In my quest for an ultimate justification for the application of the rule, I thus face an infinite regress of rule-formulations on rule-formulations, new interpretations of the rule that show my action to be in conformity with the original rule. Accordingly, the discussion culminates in the famous rule-following paradox and the following conclusion:

> That there is a misunderstanding here is shown by the mere fact that in this chain of reasoning we place one interpretation behind another, as if each one contented us at least for a moment, until we thought of yet another lying behind it. For what we thereby show is that there is a way of grasping a rule which is *not* an interpretation, but which, from case to case of application, is exhibited in what we call "following the rule" and "going against it." (PI §201)

By "interpretation" Wittgenstein means a rule-formulation, namely, an explicit, conceptual expression of the rule: "One should speak of interpretation only when one expression of a rule is substituted for another" (PI §201). Such rule-formulations do not fix unequivocally the norm of application, because, just like aesthetic reasons, "they are in the nature of further descriptions" of the original rule (LC 9:30).

So if the mistake underlying the paradox is to equate understanding with an interpretation, available to the speaker in the form of an explicit rule-formulation, then what else is left? What does it mean to grasp the rule in a way that is not an interpretation but not mere empirical regularity of behavior either? Wittgenstein's initial reply is formulated by reference to the notion of a practice: "That's why 'following a rule' is a practice. And to *think* one is following a rule is not to follow a rule. And that's why it's not possible to follow a rule 'privately'; otherwise, thinking one was following a rule would be the same thing as following it" (PI §202). However, without further explication, the appeal to practice is open to various interpretations ranging from a reduction of linguistic norms to practical utility to Kripke's skeptical solution, namely, that there is no norm beyond the consensus of the community upholding assert-ability conditions (Kripke 1982, 74–79). Yet, neither language-independent practices, nor communal consensus will explain the notion of understanding. Consensus is an empirical, statistical notion, whereas understanding is a normative one (PI §241).

Unlike causes, the chains of which continue indefinitely, reasons come to an end. According to Wittgenstein, "Once I have exhausted the justifications, I have reached bedrock, and my spade is turned. Then I am inclined to say: 'This is simply what I do'" (PI §217; see PI §§326, 482, 485). While there *is* a scope of justifications available both in aesthetics and in language, these will soon run out. In a way reminiscent of the *Tractatus*'s imagery of logic as the ineffable limit of language, Wittgenstein characterizes the end of justifications as a boundary: "A reason can only be given within a game. The links of a chain of reasons come to an end, at the boundary of the game." (PG, 97; see PI §§119, 499). At the boundary of the game there is no further justification to be found, nor any room to meaningfully question whether one ought to follow the rule. Instead, "when I follow the rule, I do not choose. I follow the rule *blindly*" (PI §219). So what should we make of this bedrock, where my grasp of the rule takes a form other than interpretation, where I follow the rule but do so *blindly*?

We have encountered a similar boundary of justifications in Wittgenstein's discussion on aesthetic judgments. I can give reasons for my judgment by comparisons and further descriptions of the aesthetic phenomenon; some justi-fications are closer to a calculation, as the case of demonstrating the necessity of a note by writing out the tune in chords (LC 9:39; BBB, 15; LA II:13). But as argued here, after such explanations are given, they must "appeal to you," "satisfy you," "click" for you – you must *see* the note's necessity, say, for yourself (LC 9:31; LA III:1–4, 10). For the explanation to become a reason for you in the sense in which we are expected to know our motives for action, you must personally endorse it (LC 9:31; LA III:12). The "appeal" in question is not a psychological notion, but already incorporates a normative pull: you "try to clear up circumstances; & in the end what you say will <u>appeal to</u> the judge" (LC 9:32). But if, in spite of my efforts to demonstrate the note's necessity, "it does not appeal to you, there is an end" (LC 9:31). Taking my lead from Wittgenstein's statement that the understanding of a sentence is like the understanding of a musical tune, I want to suggest that this "end" of aesthetic reasons gives us the most viable model for what he means by blind rule-following.

Wittgenstein is not the first to ask how it is possible to apply a rule to a particular case. Nor is he the first to connect the moment of blind rule-following (i.e. rule-following without a conceptually formulated justification), to practice and to aesthetic judgment. We find a version of the rule-following problem already in Kant's *First Critique* (CPR A132–136/B171–175). Moreover, as some commentators have noted, Wittgenstein's rule-following paradox resembles Kant's treatment of the problem.[52] Indeed, the theme is as central for Kant as it is for Wittgenstein. This is because, in every cognitive judgment, a general rule, which for Kant is typically a concept, is applied to a sensible intuition. Without intuitions, concepts are empty, and without concepts, intuitions remain *blind*, as he famously states (CPR B75). Understanding as the faculty of rules is not yet capable of applying those rules to concrete particulars, because to justify the application of a rule by reference to a further rule will only lead to an infinite regress (CPR A133). Hence, Kant claims, in order to apply the rules *in concreto* and to distinguish which particulars fall under their scope, understanding needs help from the power of judgment, which, in the *First Critique*, is introduced as the faculty of subsuming intuitions under conceptual rules. The power of judgment is developed by concrete training and by means of examples. But while training and the imitation of others can provide a "limited understanding of the rules," ultimately "the faculty of making use of them correctly must belong to the student himself" (CPR A133).

Now consider the student in the *Investigations*, learning the rule governing the series of natural numbers. Wittgenstein writes: "At first, perhaps, we guide his hand in writing out the series 0 to 9; but then the *possibility of communication* will depend on his going on to write it down by himself" (PI §143). He continues: "Let us suppose that after some efforts on the teacher's part he continues the series correctly, that is, as we do it. So now we can say that

---

[52] See Cavell 1969, 88–96; Bell 1987; Glock 1996, 326; Haugeland 1998, fn 4; Eldridge 2004; McDowell 2009, 110; Baz 2016.

he has mastered the system." (PI §145) Wittgenstein's characterization of rule-following as a practical ability and his emphasis on training reflect Kant's portrayal of the role of the power of judgment in the *First Critique* (PI §§6, 150). And, like Kant, Wittgenstein gives examples an indispensable role in the transmission of rules: "If a person has not yet got the *concepts*, I'll teach him to use the words by means of *examples* and by *exercises*. – And when I do this, I do not communicate less to him than I know myself" (PI §208).

What makes the parallel between Kant and Wittgenstein significant is that Kant's mature treatment of his rule-following problem is intertwined with his account of the judgment of beauty. In Kant's *First Critique*, the power of judgment is given just a supporting if necessary role in the formation of cognitive judgments. In the *Third Critique*, a work dedicated to the faculty that is supposed to bridge the gap between the conceptual rule and its particular instance, Kant returns to the rule-following problem (CPJ 5:168–169). Describing the typical use of the power of judgment in which a particular intuition is subsumed under a known rule as determining, he notes that, in addition to its determining use, the power of judgment can be used reflectively. This is the case when our judgment begins from the particular without having a conceptual rule ready at hand, and yet sees the particular as a unified whole. Judgments of beauty have a special place among reflective judgments, because they are "blind" in the exact sense of neither presupposing nor leading to concepts (CPR B75; CPJ 5:221). It is precisely for this reason that the judgment of beauty escapes the lurking regress of conceptual justification for the application of a conceptual rule that cognitive judgments face.

At this point, one might object that escaping the regress of conceptual justifications is not much comfort if we fall back on something as foggy as aesthetic judgment. Surely such a move must undermine Wittgenstein's core commitment to the normativity of grammar, not to mention conflict with his rejection of a private language. The concern would indeed be warranted if Wittgenstein's account of aesthetic judgment were empiricist, reducing the aesthetic judgment to mere feelings of approbation. However, as argued in Section 3.2, Wittgenstein rejects just such a view in favor of the Kantian conception of aesthetic judgment, which assumes that pure aesthetic judgments are universally valid and make a justified claim to necessity in spite of relying on feeling. Even without an established conceptual rule, the judgment of beauty is offered "as an example of a universal rule that one cannot produce" in the form of an explicit rule-formulation (CPJ 5:237).

What Kant is ultimately after in the *Third Critique* is reassurance of our *right* to think of "the particular as contained under the universal" when the fit between the general conceptual rule and the sensible particular cannot be justified by appeal to further concepts (CPJ 5:179). Cognitive judgments need not remain paralyzed in the face of the infinite regress of rules on the application of rules, because the particular intuition and the concept are united by a *feeling* of appropriateness – a feeling that finds its paradigmatic manifestation in a judgment of beauty. This is why Kant claims that in a judgment of beauty we find something that is "requisite for possible cognitions in general" (CPJ 5:290; see CPJ 5:286–287).[53]

A point that often goes unnoticed is that the sections usually treated as Wittgenstein's discussion of how the rule can determine its correct application are immediately preceded by a remark on music (PI §§185–242). In section 184, Wittgenstein gives a musical version of the more well-known mathematical example of the rule-following problem (PI §§143–149). He writes:

> I want to remember a tune, and it escapes me; suddenly I say "Now I know it," and I sing it. What was it like suddenly to know it? Surely it can't have occurred to me *in its entirety* in that moment! – Perhaps you will say: "It's a particular feeling, as if it were now *there*" – but *is* it now there? Suppose I then begin to sing it and get stuck? – But may I not have been *certain* at that moment that I knew it? So in some sense or other it was *there* after all! – But in what sense? Perhaps you would say that the tune was there if, for example, someone sang it through, or rehearsed it in his imagination from beginning to end. I am not, of course, denying that the statement that the tune is there can also be given a quite different sense – for example, that I have a bit of paper on which it is written. (PI §184)

The challenge of knowing the tune is in many ways like that of grasping the rule determining the series of natural numbers (PI §143). Individual performances of the tune are, as it were, applications of the rule that determines whether a particular performance counts as a performance of that tune (just as the rule constituting the use of the word "table" determines what particular things are correctly called tables). Also Wittgenstein candidates for the criterion of knowing the tune – a particular feeling, performance, a mental image, etc. – to be rejected as unsuccessful, correspond to the mathematical example (see PI §§147–155).

But importantly, the example of the tune immediately evokes the moment at which justifications given by rule-formulations come to an end. For what would a rephrase or an alternative expression of the tune, given as an interpretation of the original, look like? While I can try and justify my claim to knowledge of the tune by writing it down on the bit of paper Wittgenstein mentions or by analyzing the tune in terms of tonal functions, such explanations capture the

---

[53] On the contribution of reflective judgment in cognition, see, for example, Bell 1987; Ginsborg 1997; Allison 2001, 150–155, 176–177.

tune in a "quite different sense" (PI §184). For to know a tune is also to have a hold of its internal, purposive unity, to have a grasp of the "completeness of the tune" (NB, 40).

Later in the text, Wittgenstein returns to the parallel between understanding a sentence and a musical tune, offering a revised version of the *Brown Book* remark:

> Understanding a sentence in language is much more akin to understanding a theme in music than one may think. What I mean is that understanding a spoken sentence is closer than one thinks to what is ordinarily called understanding a musical theme. Why is just *this* the pattern of variation in intensity and tempo? One would like to say "Because I know what it all means." But what does it mean? I'd not be able to say. As an "explanation," I could compare it with something else which has the same rhythm (I mean the same pattern). (PI §527)

The import of the remark is threefold. First, music and language alike are systems constituted by autonomous rules that cannot be justified by reference to something external to those systems. Second, my understanding of a specific expression (a chord, cadence, tune, word, or sentence) requires mastery of those rules. Without such mastery, my responses will be like those of a dog that "wags its tail when music is played" (LA I:17). And yet, third, that understanding cannot be exhaustively explained by explicit rule-formulations, nor derived from them. In language and music alike, I will reach a point where explanations come to an end, where "I'd not be able to *say*" (PI §527; emphasis added). After the explanations, examples, and exercises that are part of my immersion into the rules of grammar have been exhausted, my ability to judge requires that I "develop a feeling for the rules" (LA I:15). I must learn to *feel* how the general rule fits the particular case just as I "learn to *feel* the ending of a church mode as an ending" (PI §535; see PI §292). This feeling is indispensable for my ability to hear the musical tune as a complete whole, whose parts "click" into place and become a meaningful pattern for me. What I am suggesting, then, is that here we have a case of understanding (i.e. of grasping a rule), that is not an interpretation if by interpretation we mean an explicit, conceptual rule-formulation.

As argued by David Bell, Wittgenstein's appeal to music in relation to the rule-following paradox is not incidental, but intended to do work similar to that Kant assigns to reflective judgment.[54] This is to say that the resolution to the rule-following problem appeals to the two perspectives introduced and elaborated in Kant's *Third Critique*, the determining (discursive, transitive) and the reflective (intuitive, intransitive) perspective. In Section 2.3, I argued that these

---

[54] Bell 1987, 239–244; see also Moore 2007 and 2011.

two perspectives are present already in Wittgenstein's early philosophy. In his later philosophy, they resurface in his distinction between the two uses of the word "understanding" that, according to him, "make up my *concept* of understanding" (PI §532):

> We speak of understanding a sentence in the sense in which it can be replaced by another which says the same; but also in the sense in which it cannot be replaced by any other. (Any more than one musical theme can be replaced by another.)
>
> In the one case, the thought in the sentence is what is common to different sentences; in the other, something that is expressed only by these words in these positions. (Understanding a poem.) (PI §531)

The first, transitive case of understanding corresponds to the case of having an explicit explanation of the meaning of the sentence ready at hand, to be given as an interpretation. In Kantian terms, my understanding stems from the determining use of the power of judgment which subsumes a particular instance under a known conceptual rule. In the second, intransitive case I have exhausted such explanations and follow the rule without a further conceptual justification. This type of understanding arises from the reflective use of the power of judgment that shows its object – in this case a sentence – as a meaningful, purposive whole in spite of my inability to further explain what that meaning or purpose is, any more than I can explain what a musical theme or a poem, which I experience as meaningful, really means (see CPJ 5:405–410).

Katalin Makkai has recently argued that Bell is mistaken to assume that Kant and Wittgenstein take a feeling for the applicability of a rule to a particular to end the regress of rules. Claiming that the feeling thus postulated is not a proper act of judging but an "object of fantasy," she argues that Bell's interpretation leads to an illusory notion of self-determining rules (Makkai 2021, 54). Without a "separate explanation or elaboration," an immediate act of seeing or feeling cannot "bear the explanatory weight for which it is invoked," which is what Wittgenstein, on Makkai's reading, aims to expose (56).[55] In my view, Wittgenstein's attention to aesthetic judgment, and especially its difference from merely subjective feelings, is meant to provide just the sort of separate explanation of the validity of a judgment grounded in a feeling that Makkai finds missing. Makkai's argument relies on the claim that the feeling of the applicability of a rule is not a proper act of judging (54). But the aesthetic judgment *is* an act of judging, albeit one that involves no concepts and hence is "blind" in Kant's sense of the term. Moreover, since aesthetic judgment

---

[55] For another critical take on Bell's argument, see Sullivan 2011.

involves reasons which I must personally endorse, blind rule-following does not entail that "I am relieved of responsibility" as Makkai suggests (60).

Just as an aesthetic judgment is not detached from their object, intransitive understanding of a sentence, manifest in seeing or feeling the form of the sentence, is not detached from the rules of grammar. It is not a causally induced response to the sentence, where no norms are involved (PI §289). The point is rather that, at the boundary of the game, I do not look for yet another justification, but rely on my feeling of the formal purposiveness of the rule-governed language-game as a whole. It makes no sense to ask for a justification for the grammatical proposition "Every rod has a length," as this is what I must take for granted in the game of measuring (PI §251). Yet I may experience the clicking together of the parts of that game and come to see how the grammatical proposition is, as it were, the missing piece of the puzzle. It makes the game complete in a way that allows for the realization of various purposes *within* the game, in spite of having no purpose to be established from *without*. The situation is like grasping the necessity of the note as part of a melody. While I must *see* or *hear* that necessity, this can only happen by turning my attention to the formal features of the melody made possible by the rules of the musical system. This formalistic emphasis on shared rules is vital for the possibility of communication. And while there is more room for disagreement in the domain of aesthetics in comparison to measuring, say, we must accept something as a given in both cases. If you fail to see the unshakeable certainty of "Every rod has a length" or refuse to accept that "This is where the cadence comes to an end," our possibility of understanding one another soon comes to an end.[56]

To sum up, if understanding is a normative notion, then the rules constitutive of the meaning of a sentence must be part of my reason for using the sentence in a particular way. But in my attempt to justify my application of the rule by reference to new expression of the rule, I face an infinite regress of rule-formulations. In order to stop that regress, we need a "way of grasping a rule which is *not* an interpretation," but is not a merely subjective reaction either (PI § 201). Without such blind rule-following, we will either launch on the afore-mentioned regress or else fall back on a naturalistic model of understanding that is unacceptable for Wittgenstein. I have argued that in aesthetic judgment we find precisely the kind of grasp of a rule which is not an interpretation, and which brings together the rule and in its application in a nonconceptual yet normative manner. The "necessity" we experience when hearing one musical thought following another or a particular note as an indispensable element of

---

[56] Cavell has argued that this "given" could be seen as playing a role similar to what Kant, in the *Third Critique*, assigns to "common sense" as the prerequisite of "universal communicability" (CPJ 5:238–239; see Cavell 1969, 88–96; 1979, 30–32).

a melody is not reducible to facts of nature. Nor can it be reduced to practical utility. Rather, the necessity arises out of the system as a whole, which I cannot prescribe from without but can simply describe and illuminate by comparisons. Ultimately, though, you must see it for yourself.

## 5 Aesthetics and Philosophy

In his lectures on aesthetics, Wittgenstein dedicates most of his attention to aesthetic judgments and explanations. He argues that aesthetic explanations are not causal. They do not appeal to the artist's or the audience's mental states, nor do they explain the arts by reference to nature, art's cognitive gains, or practical utility. The relevant kinds of explanations are further descriptions of the object of aesthetic appreciation or comparisons between the object and something else. Such descriptions and comparisons aim at drawing attention to the features of the object itself. They aim at showing it from a perspective that makes the features of the object "click," even when we cannot explain what it is that "clicks" and why (LA III:5).

In spite of maintaining that there is no objective, discursively explicable paradigm to serve as the ultimate criterion of aesthetic "correctness," Wittgenstein uses normative terminology throughout his remarks on aesthetics. He describes aesthetic systems as being constituted by rules and hence meriting "grammatical" investigation. And he claims that our aesthetic judgments commit us: they are not mere expressions of subjective feelings but call for justification. The justifications have the character of reasons and they are given to compel another to see the aesthetic phenomenon in a particular way. Finally, for the explanation to appeal to you and to become a reason for you, you must *see* or *feel* the "click" between a particular feature and the system. In this respect, the grasp of the "necessity," "rightness," or "wrongness" of an aesthetic feature involves an irreducibly subjective moment of endorsement.

In 1933, Wittgenstein asks: "Are the same sort of reasons given elsewhere except in Ethics?" His answer is: "Yes; in philosophy" (LC 9:32). The obvious similarity between aesthetics and philosophy is that for Wittgenstein, just as for Kant, both are qualitatively different from natural sciences. Both Kant and Wittgenstein argue that philosophical illusions, manifest most notably in metaphysics, arise from our failure to properly distinguish between factual statements and the conditions of those statements (BBB, 18; RPP I:949; Z §458; PI §90; CPR A295–302/B352–359). For the early Wittgenstein, this means a failure to distinguish between the form and content of language; for the later Wittgenstein, between what people say and the grammar that makes saying something possible (TLP 3.323–3.33, 4.113–4.1212; PI §240–242).

That philosophy does not aim at establishing new facts but turns to reflect the possibility of that which we already know is one of Wittgenstein's most firmly held beliefs from the very beginning. In the *Tractatus*, he states that "philosophy is not a body of doctrine, but an activity"; it "does not result in 'philosophical propositions,' but rather in the clarification of propositions" (TLP 4.112; see TLP 4.0031; CPR A11–12/B24–26). And he reaffirms the correctness of his view in the *Investigations*, noting that "It was correct to say that our consider-ations must not be scientific ones.... All *explanation* must disappear, and description alone must take its place" (PI §109; see TLP 4.111; LWL, 73–74; PI §§124–128).

As in aesthetics, where the investigation begins from an aesthetic puzzle like "Why is this note absolutely necessary?," a philosophical puzzle arises from our failure to grasp the "forms of language" (PI §111). A description of the musical context of the note or of the language-game to which a word belongs allows us to see how the note or the word contributes to the overall structure of that organized whole (PI §§23, 43, 108). And just as in aesthetics, where an apt comparison allows us to see how the pieces of the aesthetic puzzle fit together, so too in philosophy the right object of comparison may reveal the source of our philosophical confusion (PI §§130–131). The perspective or "overview" we acquire from grammatical investigation reveals the similarities and differences between language-games, but also the difference between what people say and what they take for granted (PI §§122, 241–242). Instead of giving a reductionist explanation of language, the resulting "surveyable representation produces precisely that kind of understanding which consists in 'seeing connections'" (PI §122). This sort of understanding we have, of course, encountered in Wittgenstein's treatment of aesthetic judgment.[57]

One of the first commentators to draw attention to the "queer resemblance between a philosophical investigation … and one in aesthetics" was Stanley Cavell (CV, 29 [25]).[58] In his seminal "Aesthetic Problems of Modern Philosophy," Cavell argues that the claims of ordinary language philosophers, who for him represent the followers of Wittgenstein's later philosophy, should be seen against the model of aesthetic judgment as understood by Kant. Instead of resting on conclusive arguments, philosophical claims about language are invitations to see the object of investigation in a certain way. As such, they appeal to a kind of attunement between us. This attunement, that is, our

---

[57] On the connection between aesthetics and the descriptive method, see, for example, Kuusela 2017; Schulte 2018; Moyal-Sharrock 2020.

[58] Cavell's work has heavily influenced the reception of Wittgenstein's philosophy and aesthetics especially in North America. See, for example, Gibson and Huemer, 2004; Friedlander 2011a; Hagberg 2008, 2018; Hagberg 2017; Sedivy 2016; Makkai 2021.

"agreement in definitions [and] judgments that is required for communication," Cavell connects to Kant's "universal communicability" (PI §242; see Cavell 1969, 88–96; Cavell 1979, 30–32; CPJ 5:239).

It is important to notice that the consequences of Cavell's proposal look quite different if the parallel between aesthetics and philosophy is not read in light of Kant's aesthetics. If we overlook Kant's emphasis on form as the shared object of aesthetic attention, the importance of "seeing for oneself" may look like an invitation to consider only the "musicality of language" at the expense of its "systematicity and normativity" (see Day 2017, 23). This, in turn, may lead to the view that grammatical relations are not "established or grounded by any-thing beyond the experience of connection itself," in other words, that rules and their applications are not internally related in the strict sense of the word (19; see 5fn 2, 19fn19). But, as I have argued, not every instance of rule-following is fruitfully illuminated by reference to aesthetics. Intransitive understanding, modelled after aesthetic judgment, becomes pertinent in quite specific cases, the most prominent being philosophy, ethics, aesthetics, mathematics, and religion – a list reminiscent of the Tractarian ineffabilia. I do not find it incidental that Cavell himself focuses on the claims of ordinary language *philosophers*. If one treats grammatical investigation as a form of transcenden-tal investigation, as Cavell does, then one is unlikely to overlook the difference between philosophical and ordinary, empirical claims (Cavell 1969, 64, 90).

Without due attention to the nonconceptuality of aesthetic judgment, in turn, we open the door to the infinite regress of conceptually formulated rules. This is the risk in equating aesthetic judgment too directly with aspect-seeing. Granted, aesthetics and aspect-seeing appear in close proximity in Wittgenstein's work and have significant points of overlap.[59] Like beauty, an aspect is not a "property of an object" (PPF §247 [PI, xi, 212]). Both are a matter of *seeing* rather than knowing, and both have the capacity to "put our attunement with other people to the test" (Baz 2000, 99). Finally, an aesthetic judgment may sometimes presuppose something like seeing an aspect, as when we hear a few bars of music as an introduction to what follows or when we find the right accentuation for reading a poem (PPF §§178, 209 [PI, xi, pp. 202, 206]; LA I:12).[60] Yet, I would be cautious to equate the two. Seeing the duck in the duck–rabbit picture need not be satisfying in the way in which finding the right tempo for a musical performance is. And it would be odd to say that when the right tempo is found, we have found an aspect of the performance that we can then change at will, which is what aspect-seeing allows (PPF §256 [PI, xi, 213]).

---

[59] See, for example, BBB, 162ff; PPF §§111–364 [PI, xi]; RPP1 §§507, 545–546, 1130.

[60] On aesthetics and aspect-seeing, see Baz 2000; Rowe 2004; Schulte 2004; Batkin 2010; Kemp and Mras 2016.

Unlike the duck–rabbit picture, which stays the same while my impression of it changes, the musical performance itself changes together with its tempo (PPF §§130–131, 152 [PI, xi, pp. 196, 199]).

Drawing on Cavell, Avner Baz has explored Wittgenstein's aspect-seeing as a model for bringing together a concept and a particular. While acknowledging the parallel, he argues that to expand Kant's account of beauty to aspect-seeing would be to "aestheticize ... our ordinary and normal relation to our world" (Baz 2016, 619). I agree, but on grounds different from Baz's. Unlike Baz, who denies the conceptuality of aspects, I take at least some aspects to be dependent on the conceptual (see Baz 2020, 10–19). As Wittgenstein notes, "Sometimes the conceptual is dominant in an aspect" (LW1 §582; see RPP1 §§70–74; PPF §§139–140, 144 [PI, xi, 197]). However, this need not render the perception of an aspect "objective," at least if we take our lead from Kant as Baz does. This is because the judgment of beauty is not, *pace* Baz, the only judgment Kant takes to fall between objective empirical judgments and merely subjective likings (cf. Baz 2016, 612). Teleological judgments are not objective in the sense of determining particulars under given concepts. Yet, they involve concepts as they attribute purposes to natural organisms. But for Kant, purposes are not objective properties: it looks *as if* the purpose of the heart is to pump blood, but from the viewpoint of theoretical reason we cannot claim to *know* this (CPJ 5:360–361; 5:370). This "as if" quality of teleological judgments and their unique relation to concepts, might make them a more suitable point of comparison for Wittgenstein's aspects as an "intermediate link" between aesthetic judgments and ordinary empirical judgments (PI §122).

On my reading, the roots of the parallel between philosophy and aesthetics and accordingly of the notion of a surveyable representation lie in Wittgenstein's early idea of the *sub specie aeterni* perspective that shows its object as a limited whole. In 1930, Wittgenstein connects the *sub specie aeterni* perspective to a mode of thought, characterized in a way reminiscent of surveyable representation:

> But now it seems to me too that besides the work of the artist there is another through which the world may be captured sub specie aeterni. It is – as I believe – the way of thought which as it were flies above the world and leaves it the way it is, contemplating it from above in its flight. (CV, 7 [5])

In 1933, Wittgenstein claims that philosophy aims at providing a "synopsis of many trivialities," which "enables you to overlook a system at a glance" (LC 5:29; 9:38). And he distinguishes the *intuitive* perspective that "takes something in as a whole at a glance" from a *discursive* perspective that treats language as an explicable calculus (LC 8:58). Here, too, Wittgenstein connects the intuitive perspective to aesthetics explicitly. According to him, "There's no such thing as an immediate recognition of an hypothesis ~~as an hypothesis~~; but there is an immediate pleasure in seeing a neat way of representation" (LC 9:38). This is because our "aesthetic craving for an explanation is not satisfied by a hypothesis," but only by a surveyable representation provided by a description of the system (LC 9:39). Hence, instead of explaining phenomena by reference to new facts or hypotheses, "in Mathematics, Ethics, Aesthetics, Philosophy, answer to a puzzle is to make a synopsis possible" (LC 9:39).

I argued in Section 2.3 that, in the *Tractatus*, the grasp of language involves an inexpressible moment of seeing the form shared by language and reality and connected this idea to Kant's transcendental aesthetic. As I read it, Wittgenstein's later notion of blind rule-following hits the same chord. Once we have exhausted our discursive resources of justification, we must "*look and see*" how our language-games hang together (PI §66). When discussing the pupil learning the series of natural numbers, Wittgenstein notes that "here too, our pupil's ability to learn may come to an end" (PI §143). He asks himself: "What do I mean when I say 'the pupil's ability to learn *may* come to an end here'?" (PI §144). The answer Wittgenstein gives to this question may be read as a testimony of the character of grammatical investigation in philosophy and of the way in which the resulting synopsis does philosophical work:

> Do I report it from my own experience? Of course not. (Even if I have had such experience.) Then what am I doing with that remark? After all, I'd like you to say: "Yes, it's true, one could imagine that too, that might happen too!" – But was I trying to draw someone's attention to the fact that he is able to imagine that? – I wanted to put that picture before him, and his *acceptance* of the picture consists in his now being inclined to regard a given case differently: that is, to compare it with *this* sequence of pictures. I have changed his *way of looking at things*. (Indian mathematicians: "Look at this!") (PI §144)

So it is not just in aesthetics where the goal of descriptions and comparisons is to try to get another to *see* the object of investigation from an illuminating perspective. The synoptic overview of grammar provided by philosophy similarly aims at changing our way of *looking* at things. In this respect, Wittgenstein's later conception of our relation to grammar is not all that different from his early approach to logical form.[61]

At this point, it is instructive to return to the significance of the distinction between the discursive and the intuitive perspectives for Kant's philosophical enterprise. According to Kant, the discursive perspective yields empirical

---

[61] See, for example, TLP 4.023, 6.1221, 6.2321; PI §§37, 66, 72–74, 122, 340, 401, 483, 490, 578.

knowledge by determining sensible intuitions under concepts. Such judgments belong to a causal explanation of the world, which presents the world as a mechanistic aggregate of facts (CPJ 20:217). By contrast, the intuitive perspective, manifest in reflective judgments, shows nature as a purposive whole and its organisms as functional systems. It judges them from a teleological point of view. This perspective is indispensable also for making sense of human action, intentional states, and artefacts, because these too presuppose the notion of a purpose (CPJ 5:220, 5:395–399; 5:406). Kant is careful to stress that, objectively speaking, there are no purposes in nature. Nor does the reflective perspective yield *knowledge* or warrant scientific *explanation* of nature. Given that the reflective perspective relies on the power of judgment's own principle of "formal purposiveness," also called the principle of the "lawfulness of the contingent as such," the resulting perspective only warrants the *description* [*Beschreibung*] of nature (CPJ 20:217, 5:181, 5:417).

I have argued that Kant's idea of the intuitive perspective that allows one to see formal purposiveness in the world is reflected in Wittgenstein's philosophy throughout his career. In his early work, it surfaces in the idea of a contemplation of the world as a limited whole and in the comparison between a tautology and a musical theme, which is "complete in itself" in virtue of its own form (NB, 40). In the middle period, it appears in his idea of a synoptic overview and in the idea of an aesthetic paradigm that cannot be formulated (BBB, 166; LC 9:33; LA III:5; CV, 65 [57]). However, while Kant's account accommodates the tabulation of a fixed set of a priori concepts and the formulation of a moral law, applicable to empirical reality, Wittgenstein denies the availability of such *expressible* truths and does so from the very beginning. At the same time, he acknowledges necessities we endorse as self-evident, such as the superiority of living in harmony with the contingent facts of the world, the necessity of a note having some pitch, or the unshakeable certainty of a rod having some length (NB, 78; TLP 2.0131; PI §251; RFM III §39). These necessities are formal. They are not statements about empirical reality, but features of our way of encountering the world to be uncovered by turning to look at what lies in front of our eyes.[62] In this respect, the weight Wittgenstein gives to the reflective perspective actually surpasses its role in Kant's philosophy.

Referring to Goethe's study of plants – which in Goethe's own judgment is "entirely in the spirit of [Kant's] ideas" (Cassirer 1945, 61) – Wittgenstein writes:

---

[62] On the relation between necessity and contingency in Wittgenstein and the difference with Kant, see Moore 1997, 126–136.

> Goethe in *Metamorphose der Pflanzen*, suggests that all plants are variations
> on a theme. What is the theme?
>     Goethe says "They all point to a hidden law." But you wouldn't ask: What
> is the law? <u>That</u> they point, is all there is to it. (LC 9:33)

The final remark accords with Kant's principle of the "lawfulness of the contingent as such." The lawfulness we see in beauty and in plants and other organisms
of nature cannot be explained by reference to empirical facts, as it essentially
depends on our own activity of looking at the phenomenon from the right
perspective. Returning to Goethe in 1947, Wittgenstein contrasts philosophical
investigation with factual investigation. Once again he highlights descriptions
and comparisons as essential for philosophy, and claims that Goethe aimed at
something similar. In his description of plants, Goethe aimed at showing "analogies in their structure" and thereby established a "new order among these
descriptions" (RPP I §950; see PI §§73, 90, 132; PO, 133). Instead of explaining,
he is just describing and "saying: 'Look at it like *this*'" (RPP I §950).[63]

For Wittgenstein, *looking* and *seeing* are not philosophically innocent
notions. Drawn from the aesthetic domain broadly conceived, they signify
a mode of grasping reality that cannot be pinned down by discursive explanations. Yet, as Wittgenstein's repeated instruction for philosophers to *look and
see* demonstrates, the kind of understanding they offer is vital for our grasp of
logical form and, later, grammar. This is why we cannot afford to dismiss
Wittgenstein's interest in aesthetics as a secondary preoccupation, unrelated
to the philosophical core of his work. What he has to say about aesthetics,
understood as an investigation of the domain of sensibility in general, is
indispensable for understanding the development of his conception of language
and philosophy.

---

[63] On the affinities between Wittgenstein and Goethe, see Rowe 1991; Schulte 2003; Friedlander
2011b.

# References

## Works Cited by Abbreviation

BBB    Wittgenstein, L. (1958). *The Blue and Brown Books*. Oxford: Blackwell.

CC    Wittgenstein, L. (1995). *Cambridge Letters: Correspondence with Russell, Keynes, Moore, Ramsey and Sraffa*. B. McGuinness and G. H. von Wright, eds. Oxford: Blackwell.

CPJ    Kant, I. (2000). *Critique of the Power of Judgment*. P. Guyer, ed.; P. Guyer and E. Matthews, tr. Cambridge: Cambridge University Press.

CPR    Kant, I. (1998). *Critique of Pure Reason*. P. Guyer and A. Wood, trs. and eds. Cambridge: Cambridge University Press.

CPrR    Kant, I. (1997). *Critique of Practical Reason*. M. Gregor, tr. and ed. Cambridge: Cambridge University Press.

CV    Wittgenstein, L. (1998 [1980]). *Culture and Value*. 1998 edition by G. H. von Wright, H. Nyman, and A. Pichler, eds.; P. Winch, tr. 1980 edition by G. H. von Wright and H. Nyman eds.; P. Winch, tr. Oxford: Blackwell.

G    Kant, I. (1997). *Groundwork of the Metaphysics of Morals*. M. Gregor ed. and tr. Cambridge: Cambridge University Press.

LA    Wittgenstein, L. (1966). *Lectures and Conversations on Aesthetics, Psychology and Religious Belief*. C. Barrett, ed. Berkeley: University of California Press.

LC    Wittgenstein, L. (2016). *Wittgenstein: Lectures, Cambridge 1930–1933. From the Notes of G. E. Moore*. D. Stern, B. Rogers, and G. Citron, eds. Cambridge: Cambridge University Press.

LE    Wittgenstein, L. (1974). "Lecture on Ethics." *The Philosophical Review* 74 (1), 3–12.

LW1    Wittgenstein L. (1982). *Last Writings on the Philosophy of Psychology*, vol.1. G. H. von Wright and H. Nyman, eds.; C. G. Luckhardt and M. A. E. Aue, trs. Oxford: Blackwell.

LWL    Wittgenstein, L. (1990). *Wittgenstein's Lectures, Cambridge 1930–32. From the notes of J. King and D. Lee*. D. Lee, ed. Oxford: Blackwell.

NB    Wittgenstein, L. (1961). *Notebooks 1914–1916*. G. H. von Wright and G. E. M. Anscombe, eds.; G. E. M. Anscombe, tr. Oxford: Blackwell.

P      Kant, I. (2004). *Prolegomena to Any Future Metaphysics*. G. Hatfield, tr. and ed., revised edition. Cambridge: Cambridge University Press.

PG    Wittgenstein, L. (1974). *Philosophical Grammar*. R. Rhees, ed.; A. Kenny, tr. Berkeley: University of California Press.

PI     Wittgenstein, L. (2009 [1958]). *Philosophical Investigations*. Revised 4th edition, G. E. M. Anscombe, P. M. S. Hacker, and J. Schulte, trs.; P. M. S. Hacker and J. Schulte, eds. 2nd edition, G. E. M. Anscombe and R. Rhees, eds.; G. E. M. Anscombe, tr. Oxford: Blackwell.

PO    Wittgenstein, L. (1993). *Philosophical Occasions*. J. Klagge and A. Nordmann, eds. Indianapolis, IN: Hackett.

PPF   Wittgenstein, L. (2009). "Philosophy of Psychology: A Fragment." Previously known as Part II of the *Philosophical Investigations*. In PI, 182–244.

PR    Wittgenstein, L. (1975). *Philosophical Remarks*. Rush Rhees, ed.; R. Hargreaves and R. White, trs. Oxford: Blackwell.

RFM  Wittgenstein, L. (1998). *Remarks on the Foundations of Mathematics*. G. E. M. Anscombe, R. Rhees, and G. H. von Wright, eds.; G. E. M. Anscombe, tr. Oxford: Blackwell.

RPP1  Wittgenstein, L. (1980). *Remarks on the Philosophy of Psychology*, vol.1. G. E. M. Anscombe and G. H. von Wright, eds.; G. E. M. Anscombe, tr. Oxford: Blackwell.

TLP   Wittgenstein, L. (1961). *Tractatus Logico-Philosophicus*. D. F. Pears and B. F. McGuinness, trs. London: Routledge.

Z     Wittgenstein, L. (1967). *Zettel*. G. E. M. Anscombe and G. H. von Wright, eds.; G. E. M. Anscombe, tr. Berkeley: University of California Press.

## Secondary Sources

Allen, R. and Turvey, R. (2001). *Wittgenstein, Theory and the Arts*. London: Routledge.

Allison, H. (1986). "Morality and Freedom: Kant's Reciprocity Thesis." *The Philosophical Review* 95 (3), 393–425.

Allison, H. (1990). *Kant's Theory of Freedom*. Cambridge: Cambridge University Press.

Allison, H. (2001). *Kant's Theory of Taste: A Reading of the Critique of Aesthetic Judgment*. Cambridge: Cambridge University Press.

Appelqvist, H. (2013). "Why Does Wittgenstein Say that Ethics and Aesthetics Are One and the Same?" In P. Sullivan and M. Potter, eds., *Wittgenstein's Tractatus: History and Interpretation*. Oxford: Oxford University Press, 40–58.

Appelqvist, H. (2016). "On Wittgenstein's Kantian Solution of the Problem of Philosophy." *The British Journal for the History of Philosophy* 24 (4), 697–719.

Appelqvist, H. (2017). "What Kind of Normativity is the Normativity of Grammar?" *Metaphilosophy* 48 (1–2), 123–145.

Appelqvist, H. (2018). "Wittgenstein on the Grounds of Religious Faith: A Kantian Proposal." *The European Journal of Philosophy* 26 (3), 1026–1040.

Appelqvist, H. (2019a). "Wittgenstein and Formalism: A Case Revisited." *Ápeiron: Estudios de filosofía* 10, 9–27.

Appelqvist, H. (2019b). "Beauty and Rules: Kant and Wittgenstein on the Cognitive Relevance of Aesthetics." In W. Huemer and I. Vendrell Ferran, eds., *Beauty: New Essays in Aesthetics and the Philosophy of Art*. Munich: Philsophia Verlag, 43–70.

Appelqvist, H. and Pöykkö, P. (2020). "Wittgenstein and Levinas on the Transcendentality of Ethics." In H. Appelqvist, ed., *Wittgenstein and the Limits of Language*. New York: Routledge, 65–89.

Arbo, A., Le Du, M. and Plaud, S. (2012). *Wittgenstein and Aesthetics: Perspectives and Debates*. Frankfurt: Ontos Verlag.

Baker, G. P. and Hacker, P. M. S. (2009). *Wittgenstein: Rules, Grammar and Necessity. Essays and Exegesis of §§185–242*, 2nd, extensively revised edition by P. M. S. Hacker. Oxford: Blackwell.

Barrett, C. (1984). "'(Ethics and Aesthetics Are One)'?" In R. Haller, ed., *Aesthetics: Proceedings of the 8th International Wittgenstein Symposium*. Vienna: Holde-Pichler-Tempsky, 17–22.

Barrett, C. (1991) *Wittgenstein on Ethics and Religious Belief*. Oxford: Blackwell.

Batkin, N. (2010). "Aesthetic Analogies." In W. and V. Krebs, eds., *Seeing Wittgenstein Anew: New Essays on Aspect-Seeing*. Cambridge: Cambridge University Press, 23–39.

Baumgarten, A. (1954). *Reflections on Poetry: Meditationes philosophicae de nonnullis ad poema pertinentibus*. K. Aschenbrenner and W. B. Holther, trs. Berkeley: University of California Press.

Baz, A. (2000). "What's the Point of Seeing Aspects?." *Philosophical Investigations* 23 (3), 97–121.

Baz, A. (2016). "The Sound of Bedrock: Lines of Grammar between Kant, Wittgenstein, and Cavell." *The European Journal of Philosophy* 24 (3), 607–628.

Baz, A. (2020). *Wittgenstein on Aspect Perception*. Cambridge: Cambridge University Press.

Bell, D. (1987). "The Art of Judgment." *Mind* 96 (382), 221–244.

Budd, M. (2011). "Wittgenstein on Aesthetics." In M. McGinn and O. Kuusela, eds., *The Oxford Handbook of Wittgenstein*. Oxford: Oxford University Press, 775–795.

Cassirer, E. (1945). *Rousseau, Kant, and Goethe*. J. Gutmann, P. O. Kristeller, and J. Herman Randall Jr., trs. Princeton: Princeton University Press.

Cavell, S. (1969). *Must We Mean What We Say?* Cambridge: Cambridge University Press.

Cavell, S. (1979). *The Claim of Reason*. Oxford: Oxford University Press.

Collinson, D. (1985). "Ethics and Aesthetics Are One." *British Journal of Aesthetics* 25 (3), 266–272.

Conant, J. (2002). "The Method of the *Tractatus*." In E. H. Reck, ed., *From Frege to Wittgenstein: Perspectives on Early Analytic Philosophy*. Oxford: Oxford University Press, 374–462.

Conant, J. (2005). "What 'Ethics' in the *Tractatus* is *Not*." In D. Z. Phillips and M. von der Ruhr, eds., *Religion and Wittgenstein's Legacy*. Aldershot: Ashgate, 39–88.

Day, W. (2017). "The Aesthetic Dimension of Wittgenstein's Later Writings." In G. L. Hagberg, ed., *Wittgenstein on Aesthetic Understanding*. Cham: Palgrave Macmillan, 3–30.

Diamond, C. (1983). "Having a Rough Story about What Moral Philosophy Is." *New Literary History* 15 (1), 155–169.

Diamond, C. (1988). "Throwing Away the Ladder." *Philosophy* 63 (243), 5–27.

Diamond, C. (2000). "Ethics, Imagination, and the Method of Wittgenstein's *Tractatus*." In A. Crary and R. Read, eds., *The New Wittgenstein*. London: Routledge, 149–173.

Diamond, C. (2005). "Wittgenstein on Religious Belief: The Gulfs Between Us." In D. Z. Phillips and M. von Ruhr, eds., *Religion and Wittgenstein's Legacy*. Aldershot: Ashgate, 99–137.

Eldridge, R. (1987). "Problems and Prospects of Wittgensteinian Aesthetics." *The Journal of Aesthetics and Art Criticism* 45 (3), 251–261.

Eldridge, R. (2004). "Rotating the Axis of Our Investigation: Wittgenstein's Investigations and Hölderlin's Poetology." In J. Gibson and W. Huemer, eds., *The Literary Wittgenstein*. New York: Routledge, 211–227.

Escalera, C. C. (2012). "On Wittgenstein's Extension on the Domain of Aesthetic Education: Intransitive Knowledge and Ethics." *Journal of Aesthetic Education* 46 (3), 53–68.

Floyd, J. (1998). "Heautonomy: Kant on Reflective Judgment and Systematicity." In H. Parret, ed., *Kant's Aesthetics*. Berlin: De Gruyter, 192–218.

Floyd, J. (2000). "Wittgenstein, Mathematics and Philosophy." In A. Crary and R. Read, eds., *The New Wittgenstein*. New York: Routledge, 232–261.

Friedlander, E. (2001). *Signs of Sense: Reading Wittgenstein's Tractatus*. Cambridge, MA.: Harvard University Press.

Friedlander, E. (2011a). "Meaning Schematisms in Cavell's Kantian Reading of Wittgenstein." *Revue Internationale de Philosophie* 2 (256), 183–199.

Friedlander, E. (2011b). "Wittgenstein et Gœthe: La view des couleurs." In C. Chauviré, ed., *L'Art de Comprendre* 20.

Garver, N. (1994). *This Complicated Form of Life*. Chicago: Open Court.

Gibson, J. and Huemer, W., eds. (2004). *The Literary Wittgenstein*. New York: Routledge.

Ginsborg, H. (1997). "Lawfulness without a Law: Kant on the Free Play of Imagination and Understanding." *Philosophical Topics* 25 (1), 37–81.

Glock, H. (1992). "Cambridge, Jena, or Vienna? The Roots of the *Tractatus*." *Ratio* 5 (1), 1–23.

Glock, H. (1996). *A Wittgenstein Dictionary*. Oxford: Blackwell.

Glock, H. (1997). "Kant and Wittgenstein: Philosophy, Necessity and Representation." *International Journal of Philosophical Studies* 5 (2), 285–305.

Glock, H. (1999). "Schopenhauer and Wittgenstein: Language as Representation and Will." In C. Janaway., ed., *The Cambridge Companion to Schopenhauer*. Cambridge: Cambridge University Press, 422–458.

Gmür, F. (2000). *Ästhetik bei Wittgenstein: Über Sagen und Zeigen*. Freiburg: Alber.

Guter, E. (2015). "The Good, the Bad, and the Vacuous: Wittgenstein on Modern and Future Musics." *The Journal of Aesthetics and Art Criticism* 73 (4), 425–439.

Guter, E. (2017). "Wittgenstein on Musical Depth and Our Knowledge of the Humankind." In G. Hagberg, ed., *Wittgenstein on Aesthetic Understanding*. Cham: Palgrave Macmillan, 217–247.

Guter, E. (2020). "The Philosophical Significance of Wittgenstein's Experiments on Rhythm." *Estetika: The European Journal of Aesthetics* 57 (1), 28–43.

Guyer, P. (1997). *Kant and the Claims of Taste.* Cambridge: Cambridge University Press.

Guyer, P. and A. Wood (2000). "Editors' Introduction." In CPJ, xiii–lii.

Hacker, P. M. S. (1986). *Insight and Illusion,* 2nd revised ed. Oxford: Oxford University Press.

Hacker, P. M. S. (2001). "Wittgenstein and the Autonomy of Humanistic Understanding." In R. Allen and M. Turvey, eds., *Wittgenstein, Theory and the Arts.* London: Routledge, 39–74.

Hagberg, G. L. (1995). *Art as Language: Wittgenstein, Meaning, and Aesthetic Theory.* Ithaca, NY: Cornell University Press.

Hagberg, G. L. (2008). *Describing Ourselves: Wittgenstein and Autobiographical Consciousness.* Oxford: Clarendon Press.

Hagberg, G. L., ed. (2017). *Wittgenstein on Aesthetic Understanding.* Cham: Palgrave Macmillan.

Hagberg, G. L., ed. (2018). *Stanley Cavell on Aesthetic Understanding.* Cham: Palgrave Macmillan.

Hanfling, O. (2004). "Wittgenstein on Music and Language." In P. Lewis, ed., *Wittgenstein, Aesthetics and Philosophy.* Aldershot: Ashgate, 151–162.

Hanslick, E. (1986). *On the Musically Beautiful.* G. Payzant, tr. and ed. Indianapolis, IN: Hackett.

Haugeland, J. (1998). "Truth and Rule-Following." In Haugeland *Having Thought.* Cambridge, MA: Harvard University Press, 305–361.

Huemer, W. (2013). "The Character of a Name: Wittgenstein's Remarks on Shakespeare." In S. Brum W. Huemer, and D. Steuer, eds., *Wittgenstein Reading.* Berlin: De Gruyter, 23–37.

Hyman, J. (2001). "The Urn and the Chamber Pot." In R. Allen and M. Turvey, eds., *Wittgenstein, Theory and the Arts.* London: Routledge, 137–152.

Jacquette, D. (2017). "Wittgenstein and Schopenhauer." In H. Glock and J. Hyman, eds., *A Companion to Wittgenstein.* Oxford: Blackwell, 57–73.

Janik, A. (1989). *Style, Politics and the Future of Philosophy.* Dordrecht: Kluwer.

Janik, A. (2007). "Das Ästhetische im Ethischen und das Ethische im Ästhetischen." In S. Majetschak and W. Lütterfelds, eds., *"Ethik und Ästhetik Sind Eins": Beiträge zu Wittgensteins Ästhetik und Kunsphilosophie.* Frankfurt: Peter Lang, 11–19.

Janik, A. and Toulmin, S. (1973). *Wittgenstein's Vienna.* New York: Simon and Shuster.

Johannessen, K. S. (1990). "Art, Philosophy and Intransitive Understanding." In R. Haller and J. Brandl, eds., *Wittgenstein: Towards a Re-evaluation.*

Proceedings of the 14th International Wittgenstein-Symposium, vol. 19,. Vienna: Springer Verlag, 323–333.

Johannessen, K. S., ed. (1998). *Wittgenstein and Aesthetics*. Bergen: University of Bergen.

Kannisto, H. (1986). *Thoughts and Their Subject: A Study of Wittgenstein's Tractatus*. Acta Philosophica Fennica, vol 40. Helsinki: The Philosophical Society of Finland.

Kemp, G. and Mras, G., eds. (2016). *Wollheim, Wittgenstein, and Pictorial Representation: Seeing-as and Seeing-in*. London: Routledge.

Kremer, M. (2001). "*The Purpose of* Tractarian Nonsense." *Noûs* 35 (1), 39–73.

Kripke, S. (1982). *Wittgenstein on Rules and Private Language*. Cambridge, MA: Harvard University Press.

Kuusela, O. (2017). "Wittgenstein's Comparison between Philosophy, Aesthetics and Ethics." In S. Majetschak and A. Weiberg, eds., *Aesthetics Today*. Berlin: De Gruyter, 333–348.

Langer, S. K. (1942). *Philosophy in a New Key*. Oxford: Oxford University Press.

Lewis, P. B. (1996). "Wittgenstein and 'the Tremendous Things in Art'." In K. S. Johannessen and T. Nordenstram, eds., *Wittgenstein and the Philosophy of Culture*. Vienna: Hölder-Pichler-Tempsky, 148–161.

Lewis, P. B. (1998). "Wittgenstein's Aesthetic Misunderstandings." In K. S. Johannessen, ed., *Wittgenstein and Aesthetics*. Bergen: University of Bergen, 18–38.

Lewis, P. B. (2004). *Wittgenstein, Aesthetics and Philosophy*. Burlington: Ashgate.

Lewis, P. B. (2005). "Original Nonsense: Art and Genius in Kant's aesthetic." In G. MacDonald Ross and T. McWalter, eds., *Kant and His Influence*. London: Continuum, 126–145.

Majetschak, S. and Lütterfelds, W., eds. (2007). *"Ethik und Ästhetik Sind Eins": Beiträge zu Wittgensteins Ästhetik und Kunsphilosophie*. Frankfurt: Peter Lang.

Makkai, K. (2021). *Kant's Critique of Taste: The Feeling of Life*. Cambridge: Cambridge University Press.

McDowell, J. (2009). "How Not to Read Wittgenstein's Philosophical Investigations: Brandom's Wittgenstein." In McDowell, *The Engaged Intellect: Philosophical Essays*. Cambridge, MA: Harvard University Press, 96–114.

McGuinness, B. (1988). *Wittgenstein: A Life. Young Ludwig (1889–1921)*. London: Duckworth.

Monk, R. (1990). *Ludwig Wittgenstein: The Duty of Genius*. London: Vintage.

Moore, A. W. (1987). "Beauty in the Transcendental Idealism of Kant and Wittgenstein." *British Journal of Aesthetics* 27 (2), 129–137.

Moore, A. W. (1997). *Points of View*. Oxford: Oxford University Press.

Moore, A.W. (2007). "Is the Feeling of Unity that Kant Identifies in his Third *Critique* a Type of Inexpressible Knowledge?" *Philosophy* 82 (321), 475–485.

Moore, A.W. (2011). "A Response to Sullivan." In R. Read and M. A. Lavery, eds., *Beyond the Tractatus Wars: The New Wittgenstein Debate*. New York: Routledge, 190–195.

Moore, A. W. (2013). "Was the Author of the *Tractatus* a Transcendental Idealist?." In P. Sullivan and M. Potter, eds., *Wittgenstein's Tractatus: History and Interpretation*. Oxford: Oxford University Press, 239–255.

Moyal-Sharrock, D. (2020). "Literature as the Measure of Our Lives." In H. Appelqvist, ed., *Wittgenstein and the Limits of Language*. New York: Routledge, 270–287.

Nyiri, J. C. (1982). "Wittgenstein's Later Work in Relation to Conservatism." In B. McGuinness, ed., *Wittgenstein and His Times*. Oxford: Blackwell, 44–64.

Pears, D. (1987). *The False Prison*, vol. 1. Oxford: Oxford University Press.

Proops, I. (2004). "Wittgenstein on the Substance of the World." *The European Journal of Philosophy* 12 (1), 106–126.

Rhees, R., ed. (1981). *Ludwig Wittgenstein: Personal Recollections*. Oxford: Blackwell.

Ritter, B. (2020). *Kant and Post-Tractarian Wittgenstein*. Cham: Palgrave Macmillan.

Rowe, M. (1991). "Wittgenstein and Goethe." *Philosophy* 33 (257), 283–303.

Rowe, M. (2004). "Criticism without Theory." In P. Lewis, ed., *Wittgenstein, Aesthetics and Philosophy*. Aldershot: Ashgate, 73–93.

Säätelä, S. (2002). "'Perhaps the Most Important Thing in Connection with Aesthetics': Wittgenstein on Aesthetic Reactions." *Revue Internationale de Philosophie* 1 (219), 49–72.

Säätelä, S. (2011). "From Logical Method to 'Messing About': Wittgenstein on 'Open Problems' in Mathematics." In O. Kuusela and M. McGinn, eds., *The Oxford Handbook of Wittgenstein*. Oxford: Oxford University Press, 159–178.

Schroeder, S. (2001). "The Coded-Message Model of Literature." In R. Allen and M. Turvey, eds., *Wittgenstein, Theory and the Arts*. London: Routledge, 210–228.

Schroeder, S. (2017). "Wittgenstein on Aesthetics." In H. Glock and J. Hyman, eds., *A Companion to Wittgenstein*. Oxford: Blackwell, 612–626.

Schopenhauer, A. (1969). *The World as Will and Representation*, vol I. E. F. J. Payne, tr. New York: Dover.

Schulte, J. (1989). "Aesthetic Correctness." *Revue Internationale de Philosophie* 43 (169), 298–310.

Schulte, J. (1993). *Experience and Expression. Wittgenstein's Philosophy of Psychology*. Oxford: Oxford University Press.

Schulte, J. (2003). "Goethe and Wittgenstein on Morphology." In F. Breithaupt, R. Raatzsch, and B. Kremberg, eds., *Goethe and Wittgenstein: Seeing the World's Unity in Its Variety*. Frankfurt: Peter Lang, 55–72.

Schulte, J. (2004). "'The Life of the Sign': Wittgenstein on Reading a Poem." In J. Gibson and W. Huemer, eds., *The Literary Wittgenstein*. New York: Routledge, 146–164.

Schulte, J. (2013). "Did Wittgenstein Write on Shakespeare?" *Nordic Wittgenstein Review* 2 (1), 7–32.

Schulte, J. (2018). "Wittgenstein's Remarks on Aesthetics and Their Context." In D. Stern, ed., *Wittgenstein in the 1930s: Between the* Tractatus *and the* Investigations. Cambridge: Cambridge University Press, 224–238.

Schulte, J. (2020). "'Engelmann told me . . . ' On the Aesthetic Significance of a Certain Remark by Wittgenstein." *Estetika: The European Journal of Aesthetics* 57 (1), 15–27.

Scruton, R. (2004). "Wittgenstein and the Understanding of Music." *British Journal of Aesthetics* 44 (1), 1–9.

Sedivy, S. (2016). *Beauty and the End of Art: Wittgenstein, Plurality and Perception*. London: Bloomsbury.

Sluga, H. (2011). *Wittgenstein*. Oxford: Wiley-Blackwell.

Stenius, E. (1960). *Wittgenstein's Tractatus: A Critical Exposition of Its Main Lines of Thought*. Oxford: Blackwell.

Stern, D. (1995). *Wittgenstein on Mind and Language*. Oxford: Oxford University Press.

Sullivan, P. (2011). "Synthesizing without Concepts." In R. Read and M. A. Lavery, eds., *Beyond the Tractatus Wars: The New Wittgenstein Debate*. New York: Routledge, 171–189.

Szabados, B. (2014). *Wittgenstein as a Philosophical Tone-Poet: Philosophy and Music in Dialogue*. Amsterdam: Rodopi.

Tam, T. (2002). "On Wonder, Appreciation, and the Tremendous in Wittgenstein's Aesthetics." *British Journal of Aesthetics* 42 (3), 310–322.

Tilghman, B. (1991). *Wittgenstein, Ethics and Aesthetics: The View from Eternity*. London: MacMillan.

Varga, S. (2009). "*Sub Specie Aeternitatis*: An Actualization of Wittgenstein on Ethics and Aesthetics." *Nordic Journal of Aesthetics* 20 (38), 35–50.

Waugh, A. (2008). *The House of Wittgenstein: A Family at War*. New York: Anchor Books.

Weininger, O. (1906). *Sex and Character*. London: William Heinemann.

Weitz, M. (1956). "The Role of Theory in Aesthetics." *The Journal of Aesthetics and Art Criticism* 15 (1), 27–35.

Wilde, C. (2004). "Ethics and Aesthetics are One." In Lewis, P. B., ed., *Wittgenstein, Aesthetics and Philosophy*. Burlington: Ashgate, 165–184.

Williams, B. (1981). "Wittgenstein and Idealism." Reprinted in Williams, *Moral Luck*. Cambridge: Cambridge University Press, 144–164.

Wittgenstein, L. (2022). *Betrachtungen zur Musik*. W. Zimmermann, ed. Berlin: Suhrkamp.

Wollheim, R. (1968). *Art and Its Objects*. New York: Harper & Row.

von Wright, G. H. (1977). "Foreword to the Edition of 1977." In CV, ix–xi [no page numbers available].

Cambridge Elements ≡

# The Philosophy of Ludwig Wittgenstein

David G. Stern

*University of Iowa*

David G. Stern is Professor of Philosophy and Collegiate Fellow in the College of Liberal Arts and Sciences at the University of Iowa. His research interests include history of analytic philosophy, philosophy of language, philosophy of mind, and philosophy of science. He is the author of *Wittgenstein's Philosophical Investigations: An Introduction* (Cambridge University Press, 2004) and *Wittgenstein on Mind and Language* (Oxford University Press, 1995), as well as more than 50 journal articles and book chapters. He is the editor of *Wittgenstein in the 1930s: Between the 'Tractatus' and the 'Investigations'* (Cambridge University Press, 2018) and a co-editor of the *Cambridge Companion to Wittgenstein* (Cambridge University Press, 2nd edition, 2018), *Wittgenstein: Lectures, Cambridge 1930–1933, from the Notes of G. E. Moore* (Cambridge University Press, 2016), and *Wittgenstein Reads Weininger* (Cambridge University Press, 2004).

## About the Series

This series provides concise and structured introductions to all the central topics in the philosophy of Ludwig Wittgenstein. The Elements are written by distinguished senior scholars and bright junior scholars with relevant expertise, producing balanced and comprehensive coverage of the full range of Wittgenstein's thought.

**Cambridge Elements ☰**

# The Philosophy of Ludwig Wittgenstein

Printed in the United States
by Baker & Taylor Publisher Services

Printed in the United States
by Baker & Taylor Publisher Services